WOKINGHAM

WOKINGHAM

A POTTED HISTORY

RICHARD GIBBS

The
History
Press

First published 2020

The History Press
97 St George's Place, Cheltenham,
Gloucestershire, GL50 3QB
www.thehistorypress.co.uk

British Library Cataloguing in Publication Data.
A catalogue record for this book is available from the British Library.

ISBN 978 0 7509 9336 4

Typesetting and origination by The History Press
Printed and bound in Great Britain by TJ International Ltd.

MIX
Paper from
responsible sources
FSC® C013056
FSC
www.fsc.org

CONTENTS

FOREWORD

In 1990 Joan and Rosemary Lea published their book *Wokingham: A Pictorial History* and in 1995 Bob Wyatt issued *Wokingham* in Budding Books' *Britain in Old Photographs* series. Although both books contain brief historical introductions, they are essentially records of Wokingham in the nineteenth and twentieth centuries as illustrated by pictures from these periods.

More recently, local historian Jim Bell has brought out *A Short History of Wokingham*, tailored to the needs of those who want a brief introduction to the town's past.

Richard Gibbs's aim has been different. Despite calling this *A Potted History*, his book is a wide-ranging conspectus of Wokingham from earliest times to the present day and he has very wisely chosen to present it thematically so that the various threads running through the story of the town can be examined one by one and not lost in general progress through the centuries.

This is not to say, however, that the individual is forgotten in favour of the overview. We are introduced to families of brewers and schoolteachers; an unusually gallant highwayman; local citizens who kindly left bequests to set up charities; a beautiful barmaid immortalised in verse; and the alderman who donated his swimming pool to the public. Bringing characters and events to life requires more than a dry recitation of facts and figures.

Richard Gibbs has risen splendidly to this challenge and has produced a thorough and much-needed account of what has driven the life and growth of Wokingham from its indistinct beginnings to the burgeoning market town it is today.

Peter Must
Chairman, The Wokingham Society
Wokingham, September 2019

INTRODUCTION

Oakingham (Wokingham). Pleasantly situated within the precincts of the forest, on the little brook called the Emme. The houses are generally built of brick and some of them make a handsome appearance, particularly that belonging to J. Roberts, Esq. lord of the one of the manors in the parish. Oakingham contains 298 houses and 1,380 inhabitants.

William Fordyce Mavor, 1813

Wokingham is located on the edge of Windsor Great Park, distanced from any large and dominating cities. It does not have a cathedral or a castle. It does not sit on any major highway or coastal harbour. It is a small market town, like hundreds of other market towns up and down the country. But this ordinariness should not be equated with a lack of history. The town has a story of its own to tell. A story of more than 1,000 years of history that is interwoven with the history of England; Wokingham reflects the quintessential English county town with its inhabitants and their dispositions, amusements and occupations.

Anyone who has lived in or visited Wokingham in the past few years has borne witness to the redevelopment of the town. Old landmarks, which can be obscured by the passage of time, can be lost entirely under the onslaught of rapid change. New arrivals to the town are less familiar with the stories and the legacies of the past. There is, therefore, the risk that the town's heritage and history are devalued or forgotten in the headlong rush for the future. Many of the things that make Wokingham a wonderful place to live and work, such as its market town trappings, can be overlooked if you don't know what to look for or where to look.

Wokingham does not have an up-to-date, unifying single coherent volume that describes the town's history. This omission is at odds with the fact that there has been detailed and scholarly research on the town's past by various local history groups and we do, in fact, possess a wonderful collection of booklets, articles and reports; Wokingham has been blessed with notable local historians from Arthur Heelas through to Ken Goatley and today's luminaries such as Jim Bell.

To try and address this deficiency, *Wokingham: A Potted History* is a primer, a summarised history of Wokingham. It can provide an overview for the reader with a general interest in the town but can also serve as a foundation for someone wishing to gain a better understanding of its past.

As with any attempt to contain nearly 1,000 years of history within a single volume, some events have been left out and others dealt with in a cursory manner. Notwithstanding these caveats, *A Potted History* hopefully provides an insight into the story of a small town in southern England.

There is a large but not substantial library of books, booklets and leaflets that cover the history of Wokingham. These serve both as a reference source for this 'potted history', and a reading list for those who want more, and more detailed information. At the end of each chapter I have added a short, list of selected references.

1

FROM EARLIEST TIMES

From earliest times a forest has existed in the south-eastern part of Berkshire, with vast stretches of heather, bracken and gorse-covered hills and moors, a wild and unfrequented region wherein deer and wolves and wild boars roamed, and British tribes dwelt, making their earthworks on the hills, a refuge for themselves and their cattle from the ravages of enemies and wild animals.

Arthur Heelas, 1928

In the far reaches of time, warm shallow waters covered much of the area surrounding present-day Wokingham. Over aeons, the gradual accumulation of the shells of tiny sea creatures laid down a bedrock of chalk. Around 50 million years ago, sharks and turtles were swimming around the mangrove swamps of a primeval ocean that deposited on its departure a thick layer of bluish clay. Millennia passed, and the area became an estuary with extensive mudflats and sandbanks formed by the ebb and flow of its tidal waters. Today these geological features are recognised by the sandy clay known as Bagshot Sands. They are a boon to some gardeners, while others are left in the proverbial mud of London clay.

And then, in the more recent geological past, the Quaternary period, from around 2 million years to 12,000 years ago, the region saw intermittent occurrences of a warm climate and ice ages. Glacial ice pushed the proto-Thames southward, and the river would erode the underlying clay, scouring the landscape. The ice would retreat, and the river would change course again and, in the process, leave behind residual deposits of gravel.

It is on one of these residual outcrops of gravel, a river terrace, that the settlement of Wokingham was established.

The town of Wokingham sits on ground that is slightly higher than the surrounding area. Market Place rises to about 70m above sea level. A pedestrian walking up the hill from where the Emm Brook crosses the Finchampstead Road, at around 45m above sea level, to the town hall, will climb 25m in less than a kilometre.

Topographically, the area around Wokingham is mainly London clay, which is overlain by the sandy Bagshot Formation. The town itself can be thought of as an island, one that is not only higher than its surroundings but also drier given its planting on a gravel outcrop.

It would be pleasing to imagine Neanderthals or early hominids strutting across this landscape chasing woolly mammoths or fleeing from sabre-toothed tigers; however, this is unlikely to have been a regular occurrence as there are only traces and hints of very early inhabitants as a result of a limited number of Palaeolithic and Neolithic finds in the area.

Around 2500 BC, the Neolithic farmers who had inhabited the British Isles for three to four millennia gave way to the new arrivals from Europe known as the Beaker people. They brought with them from Europe the understanding and technology of combining copper and tin in the right measures to make them more durable bronze instruments and tools. The Bronze Age had arrived in the UK, albeit around five centuries later than it did in ancient Greece.

In the vicinity of Wokingham, there appears to have been a small but well-established population at this time. In Barkham there are clear indications of settlements, including a curious burnt mound, reminiscent of a sauna, whose purpose is unclear.

The Beaker people also brought with them a unique culture, one feature of which literally stood out of the landscape. Their ceremonial barrows typically included luxury grave items that demonstrated the sophistication of their craftsmanship. There are notable examples of Bronze Age barrows surrounding Wokingham in Bill Hill, Bracknell and Finchampstead.

The Bronze Age eventually gave way around 800 BC to the Iron Age. The landscape that had earlier seen the construction of barrows now saw the development of hill forts such as the one nearby in Swinley Forest. The Iron

Age hill fort known incorrectly as Caesar's Camp was probably established between 500 and 300 BC, and so pre-dated any Roman influence. The only tenuous justification for the misnaming of the site by local antiquaries is that at some time it is likely to have fallen under the rule of King Cunobeline of the Catuvellauni; Cymbeline, the hero of the eponymous Shakespeare play, had been raised in Rome and was a loyal ally to the Romans.

Three Iron Age furnaces have been discovered close to the town, at what was Folly Court on the Barkham Road. At Matthewsgreen archaeologists have found a late Iron Age farmstead dating from around 40 BC. In this period, Wokingham, along with much of Berkshire, was to all intents and purposes 'the land of the Atrebates'. This Celtic tribe had fled the Roman advance in Gaul around 50 BC.

Julius Caesar invaded Britain in the winter of 55/54 BC. It was not until 43 BC that the country, or part of it, was effectively governed by the Romans and would remain under their control for the next 500 years or so, until their departure in AD 410.

The Devil's Highway, the Roman road that passes through Finchampstead on its way to Silchester or Calleva Atrebatum, is also a testament to the Roman presence. Silchester was itself a former Iron Age fort of the Atrebates tribe. Perhaps more prosaically, as further evidence of Roman occupation, there is a hoard of coins that were found at Matthewsgreen and date from the Emperor Constantine AD 306–337. The coins had been hidden, possibly by some farmer fearing assault or robbery but whom tragedy or accident overtook, thus preventing his return.

Nevertheless, despite all the indications of activity around the embryonic town, there is no tangible evidence of any permanent settlement until the fifth or sixth centuries, and even for that, it is necessary to rely on the etymology of the name Wokingham.

Numerous tribes from northern Europe filled the 'political vacuum' that was created by the departure of the Romans. The Germanic Angles and Saxons controlled, within the next 100 years after the Romans departure, much of the territory that had been under the rule of Rome; the Jutes, from Denmark, occupied some smaller areas in the south. This latest wave of invaders, and would-be settlers, imposed their language and customs on the local inhabitants, in much the same way that the Romans had. The Germanic language spoken by the Angles would eventually develop into English.

The placement of Wokingham on the gravel rise, within a heavily wooded countryside and a freshwater stream nearby, can be thought of as a deliberate act by a local Anglo-Saxon tribe called Woccingas, headed by Wocca. The Woccingas lived around the Woking area, and growth in the population could have been the impetus to encourage some members to leave the homestead to establish a new hamlet or settlement for the tribe, hence Woking – ham. Other members of the tribe decided to move further west in search of better agricultural land and settled in Woke-field.

These were turbulent times; Aidan, an Irish monk, established a monastery on Lindisfarne, and it was here in 793 that the Viking invasion began. The whole country was subjected to frequent raids and attacks. In 871, Bagsecg and Halfdan Ragnarsson camped near Reading to take on the Saxon army of Æthelwulf, the Ealdorman of the shire, in an attempt to gain control of Wessex, which included most of Berkshire. The Danes beat the Saxons back, only to be themselves beaten by Æthelwulf, who had joined forces with King Æthelred and his brother, Alfred the Great. The Danes retreated. Except for this battle, there are no other notable instances of the Viking presence in and around Wokingham; for the next 500 years or so, the small Anglo-Saxon village, most likely no more than a collection of huts in the middle of the heavily wooded forest, was undisturbed.

And then, along came the Normans and their conquest of 1066.

A group of Vikings that had settled in northern France became known as the Normans, and, by the early eleventh century, ruled a great and powerful region, sanctioned by the French Crown.

Following the death of the 'English' King, Edward the Confessor, the Normans of France, led by William (the Conqueror), sailed across the Channel and claimed the throne of England, defeating the only other contender, Harold Godwinson, at the Battle of Hastings in 1066.

When William dismissed his mercenaries in 1070, nearly all returned to France. The number who settled and remained in England was relatively few. Richard the Lionheart, King of England, Duke of Normandy, spent less than six months in England after he ascended the throne. The Norman conquerors ruled predominantly from France; England simply acquired a new ruling class.

William was pragmatic and, having conquered the country, needed to get to grips with running it as well as sharing bits out to his trusty followers.

The Anglo-Saxon Chronicle, dating from the late ninth century, states that:

… at the midwinter [1085], was the king in Gloucester with his council … After this had the king a large meeting, and very deep consultation with his council, about this land; how it was occupied, and by what sort of men. Then sent he his men over all England into each shire; commissioning them to find out 'How many hundreds of hides were in the shire, what land the king himself had, and what stock upon the land; or, what dues he ought to have by the year from the shire'.

The Domesday Book does not mention Wokingham. To put this anomaly into context, the smaller villages of Barkham, Swallowfield, Easthampstead, Finchampstead and Shinfield were all included in the survey. One explanation put forward for the omission is that, at this time, the area was included in the account of the Manor of Sonning. Roger the Priest was the Lord of the Manor as well as being the Bishop of Salisbury, and the Domesday entry for Sonning lists forty villagers, sixteen smallholders and one church. As these represented households the population is likely to have been five times larger. Having said that, by way of comparison, both Finchampstead and Swallowfield had thirty households and Barkham had ten. The listing for Sonning seems strangely deficient, or perhaps suggests that the hamlet of Wokingham was literally a couple of huts in the middle of the woods and not worth the reckoning.

Whatever the understanding or reasoning for the absence of the town from the Domesday Book, a century later, around 1190, All Saints Church was founded and dedicated by Hubert le Poore, Bishop of Salisbury.

Notwithstanding the significance of this documented event, there is some evidence that an older Chapel of Ease existed on the site.

Glebe lands are lands that the church can rent out and thus generate an income for the rectory. The Wokingham glebe lands lay to the north-west of All Saints Church. In the thirteenth century there was an ongoing dispute over the land that the church claimed, but which was being farmed by a certain Ralph the Red – Radulfus Ruffus. The church was paying rent to the Bishop of Salisbury, but received no income from it, hence their displeasure.

An enquiry was set up in 1217 by Dean Adam of Salisbury. The case was laid before Henry III's itinerant justices. The chief justice was Richard le Poore, who was ably assisted by six justices as well as the attorney Bartholomew de Kernes. Needless to say, against such opposition, in 1219, Radulfus lost the case and surrendered the land but he was allowed the use of the land for his lifetime at the rent of five shillings per annum.

John Norden's map of 1607 shows Wokingham, spelt Ockmgham, as a cluster of houses and streets around the market place. Roads or tracks lead out to Arborfield, Lodden Bridge and Easthampstead Park.

As part of the court case, it was pointed out that Stephen, who was the priest at Wokingham, had inherited the chaplaincy:

> For the whole of his life, Alfred (Alerud) the priest held, together with the Chapel of Wokingham, the land which Ralph the Red now unjustly occupies; after Alfred, his son Robert held the chapel and the land for the whole of his life, and cleared of trees a great part of that land; then came Godfrey (Godefidus) the Deacon, Alfred's son and Robert's brother; after Godfrey married, his son John in whose time the chapel was dedicated by Hubert Bishop of Salisbury (c.1190); after John came Godfrey's youngest son Stephen, who paid 40 shillings to Dean Jordan (c.1195). And so, from the time of Alfred until the time of Stephen, the land has always belonged to the chapel of Wokingham.

This convoluted family tree takes the dating of the chapel back as far as Alfred in roughly 1140, a few years before the chapel is mentioned in the Sarum Rolls of 1146. It is also clear that the priests of this chapel were not celibate, which adds weight to the argument that it is unlikely to have been established in the post-Conquest era – no self-respecting Norman overlord would establish a church and allow such carry-ons by the incumbent and obviously not celibate priest.

This provides a sound argument that the chapel most likely pre-dates the 1066 invasion. It is probable that the chapel was also associated with the monastery of Abbot Hedda in Woccingas' territory, as mentioned in a papal bull of 708 by Pope Constantine.

When Hubert le Poore died, his brother Richard, formerly the Dean of Salisbury, became Bishop and decided around 1218 to abandon the Old Sarum Cathedral for a new one in his manor of Milford by the River Avon. One way of making money in this period was the establishment of 'new towns'. Such an initiative enabled the landowner to effectively provide the equivalent of a 'tax break' to the people (burgesses) who rented the plots of land (burgage). In this instance, 'the tax breaks' amounted to not being liable for feudal duties.

Richard decided to pay for the new cathedral by creating a 'new town' in his Manor of Sonning with the purchase of a market charter for Wokingham from the Crown in 1219. It is pure speculation that during the Radulfus Ruffus court case Richard had pondered what he could do with this quiet backwater. The charter was confirmed as permanent in 1227. The market was to be held 'peaceably' every Tuesday.

In subsequent years the market would be held in Market Place, but it is likely that originally it was located in the enclosed Rose Street.

Wokingham was now clearly on the map and to make it more attractive, and lucrative for Richard; he sought and was granted in 1258 by the Crown the privilege of holding two annual fairs. The first was to be held on the 'vigil, feast and morrow' of St Barnabas, namely 10, 11 and 12 June and the second on All Saints on 31 October and 1 and 2 November.

These markets and fairs ostensibly had legitimate commercial and religious purposes, but it would not take too much to imagine that they would also be an excuse for revelry, spiced up with drinking. The stipulation in the Charter of the markets being held 'peaceably' might indicate the concern of the authorities about things getting out of hand.

Street traders would be serving 'fast food' in the form of savouries and sweetmeats of various concoctions. There would be the inns selling cheap beer. The fairs themselves would attract buyers from London in search of the plump, fatted hens for which Wokingham was renowned. There could be street entertainers from Reading or Windsor plying their trade. Cash would be exchanging hands as poultry were sold, boots were bought.

The town must have prospered over the next few decades as in 1327, when Parliament granted a tax to the king of the 'twentieth of the movable goods of every person in the realm, the clergy alone excluded', fifty-seven names of Wokingham people appeared on the roll. Among them were Geoffrey atte Beche and John Matthew, of Matthewsgreen.

The town continued to grow. By the middle of the fourteenth century there was a bell foundry in Wokingham. Wealthy men were donating to worthy causes such as John Westende, who endowed eight almshouses in 1451, in Peach Street, just opposite The Ship Inn.

The medieval town was taking shape, and much of its general layout remains today.

John Norden's map of 1607, although it is later than the medieval period, clearly shows the structure of the town before the subsequent expansion. The Market Place is discernible and both Rose Street and Peach Street can be identified. The Emm Brook is drawn, and the Barkham, Reading and Finchampstead Roads are all clearly visible; it can also be noticed that beyond this clustering of houses the surrounding countryside is sparsely populated, compared with today, with only smaller villages at Arborfield, for example.

Documents first mention Rose Street in 1289, originally Le Rothes, which can be interpreted as 'the street in the clearing'. Rose Street is an example of an enclosed medieval street, although the Broad Street end was widened in the late nineteenth century to accommodate traffic. It lays claim to some of the oldest buildings in the town, dating from the fifteenth century, including the timber-framed and jettied Wealden hall house at Nos 16–18 that at the time of writing accommodates the Wokingham and District Association for the Elderly (WADE) charity shop.

The first reference to Shute End occurs in 1321; Shute End derives from an Anglo-Saxon phrase meaning 'the land that stands out'. Peach Street or Le Peche Strete is mentioned in 1362 and is most likely named after the La Beche family. The Market Place and Broad Street were first noted in 1322. Finally, to complete the old town, there is Denmark Street (Don or Down Street), which is identified in documents dated 1407.

So, this is the design of Wokingham Old Town. In the early days of the town there were a few huts around a chapel of ease in the woods and then a street, of sorts, running westwards from All Saints Church. There were limited but productive allotments as well as a busy and hopefully peaceful market place. There was Beeches Manor House and some large halls. A narrow road went downhill towards the marshy Emm Brook and then out into the lightly wooded countryside.

Selected References

Ayres, D. (2001) 'Wokingham's Saxon Chapel – Fact or Fable?' *The Wokingham Historian,* No. 11, 10–12.

Bell, J. (2008) *St Paul's Parish Church, Wokingham.*

Berkshire Geoconservation Group (2019) Geology of Berkshire. Available at: https://berksgeoconservation.org.uk/geology.php [Accessed 27 May 2019].

British History Online (2015) *A History of the County of Berkshire.* Vol. 3, ed. P.H. Ditchfield and William Page (London, 1923) 225-236. . Available at: www.british-history.ac.uk/vch/berks/vol3/pp225-236 [Accessed 27 May 2019].

Coombs, T., Sharpe, J., Davies, H., Harrison, A., and Byard, A. (2018) 'The Land of the Atrebates: In and around Roman Berkshire', *Berkshire Archaeological Journal*, Vol. 83.

Nash Ford, D. (2001) Wokingham: 'A Town of Bells & Bull-Baiting'. *Royal Berkshire History*. Available at: www.berkshirehistory.com/villages/wokingham.html [Accessed 27 May 2019].

Neave, J. (1997) *The History of All Saints Church Wokingham.*

The Domesday Book Online (1999) Available at: www.domesdaybook.co.uk/berkshire.html [Accessed 27 May 2019].

2

STAGECOACHES AND STEAM TRAINS

WOKINGHAM COACH, from the ROSE INN, sets out every morning at seven o'clock, (Sundays excepted) and returns from The Bolt and Ton, Fleet Street, the same day at one; calls at the Gloucester Coffee-House. and White Bear, Piccadilly, both going and coming out of London. The proprietors beg leave to assure the public, that the utmost pains will be taken to accommodate them in every respect.

John Grave and Co., Proprietor, Reading Mercury, *4 November 1793*

Around 1795, the early morning scene in front of the Bush Hotel (Bush Walk), adjacent to the original Rose Inn, would have been one of hustle and bustle as the stagecoach prepared to leave for London. The horses would have been brought out from the stables at the back of the inn and harnessed up. The passengers would have been milling around, probably buying food for the day's journey. John Grave, the proprietor of the Rose, might have been busying himself, helping passengers to get aboard or cajoling his staff to get going. And then the passengers and the luggage were loaded, and the coach would pull off along Peach Street and out past All Saints Church towards London.

A century later, the railway had arrived and in 1895 the air around the train station would have been filled with the sounds of activity coming from the goods sidings a few hundred yards up from the passenger platform. There were bricks from the nearby factory on railway trucks waiting for shipment; there were barrels of beer standing ready to be loaded. In the distance, there would have been the sound of a whistle as the 8.06 steams towards Wokingham from Charing Cross heading for Reading. The steam engine roared as it passed beneath the bridge. The smoke billowed from the chimney, sending cinders and ash into the eyes of anyone who did not look away quickly enough. The stationmaster would have assisted the ladies and gentlemen onto the train and then, with a whistle and a wave of the flag, it would have been on its way.

Turnpikes and Coaches

Unlike many towns, Wokingham has not lain on some pre-existing track or path; it is not on a navigable stretch of water or a coastline. Early maps show roads into and out of the town, but they splinter and fragment into a criss-cross network of rural lanes, most fading out entirely as they come to the heaths. The Roman road that connected London and Calleva Attrebatum (Silchester) had a *mansio* in nearby Finchampstead; a *mansio* is an official stopping place on the road for messengers and other Roman officials to stop, rest and change horses. But even this road became lost to legend and known as the 'Devil's Highway' in the belief that only a supernatural being could create a road so straight.

Turnpike trusts were set up under the authority of an individual Act of Parliament to collect tolls to pay for the maintenance of primary routes across the country. Much like today, Wokingham was positioned between two of these main roads, the London to Bath and the London to Portsmouth turnpikes. The Windsor Forest turnpike connected Reading via Wokingham and Ascot to the London to Portsmouth turnpike at Virginia Water; there was also a spur to Windsor. The turnpike followed a high, sandy and dry route through the forest and came along Peach Street and out where Broad Street and the Reading Road are today.

Much like any road today, the turnpike would require continuous investment and ongoing repairs; there were tolls at Loddon Bridge and Coppid Beech to help to defray these costs. Having said that, in 1759 there was a petition to Parliament for support in making improvements to the road as:

> … the road from a place called Old Gallows, in the Parish of Sunning,
> in the County of Berks, to the Town of Wokingham and from thence
> through Sunning Hill in the County of Berks, to a stream of water or

This illustration from circa 1820 shows a stagecoach being loaded up in the galleried yard of the White Bear Inn, Piccadilly, where the Wokingham coach would arrive and depart from.

rivulet called Virginia Water in the Parish of Egham in County of Surrey, is in a very ruinous condition, narrow in many places and dangerous to travellers and cannot effectively be repaired and widened by the present methods prescribed by the law.

The relative insignificance of Wokingham at this time seems to be testified by the building of a road cutting through the Windsor Forest to the north of the town in the 1770s. The Forest Road 'bypass' was funded by public subscription and provided a shorter route from Binfield/Ascot to Reading. It seems that some people were prepared to invest in saving time to prevent going a few miles further south to Wokingham, despite the weekly markets and annual fairs.

Three stagecoaches specially serviced the town during the eighteenth century. The first stagecoach, called the Wokingham and Sunninghill Stage, started in 1756 between London and Wokingham. The start point was originally the Old Rose on Market Place, next door to The Bush. In fact, within a few years, the rivalry between the two publicans led to the starting point changing to The Bush and the development of the new and short-lived Wokingham Fly stagecoach in 1770. The third service operated from The King's Head Inn, which was adjacent to the Red Lion:

A POST-COACH sets out from the King's Head Inn, the Market-place, Wokingham, every morning (Saturdays excepted) at nine o'clock, to the Bolt-in-Tun Inn, Fleet Street, London and another Coach returns from every day at the same hour. – For conveniency of passengers the Coaches stops at the Old White Cellar and Black Bear, Piccadilly, going in and coining out.

Reading Mercury, *25 October 1790*

Post coaches were one up in terms of luxury to a stagecoach, which carried as many passengers as the law permitted. The post coach offered a better-quality ride with a limited number of passengers, and parcels, but no mail.

The coaches provided the main public form of transportation until the time of the railways. As the rail lines spread across the country Wokingham had to wait its turn to be connected to the growing network, in the interim the stagecoach continued to perform a service:

WILLIAMS's COACH FROM WOKINGHAM to the GREAT WESTERN RAILWAY STATION AT SLOUGH. PUBLIC are respect-fully informed the above Coach leaves the Bush Inn, Oakingham, at a Quarter past Seven o'clock, EVERY MONDAY, WEDNESDAY and FRIDAY Mornings … to the Slough Station, for the Train to London at Twenty Minutes before Ten; and return Oakingham the same day, after the arrival of the Train at Slough which leaves Paddington at a quarter before Five.

Reading Mercury, *13 March 1847*

Railways

There is something romantic with a touch of adventure about a steam train. Despite the nostalgia with which they are now seen, trains were at the time recognised as leading-edge technology and heralded an era of considerable change across the country, both socially and economically.

Wokingham railway station in the 1860s, a few years after it opened and before the footbridge was constructed.

Great Western Railway established the line out from Paddington and to the west of England in the 1840s. The line ran to Bristol and Bath but also brought the railway to Maidenhead and Reading by 1848. This was the start of the network expansion that would knit the country together and enable 'mass' travel as never before until the cuts introduced by Lord Beeching in the 1960s.

Wokingham station was opened in 1849 by the Reading, Guildford and Reigate Railway Company. Wokingham was the first stop out of Reading, and the next was Blackwater before the train went on to Guildford, Reigate and Redhill. The arrival of the railway in Wokingham was coincidental to the growth spurt experienced by both the brewing firms and the brick producers in the latter part of the Victorian era. It would be another decade before a station opened at Wellington College for Crowthorne in 1859.

The trains themselves were operated by the South Eastern Railway (SER) company, and in 1850 there were four daily services and three on Sundays providing access to London Paddington via Great Western Railway at Reading. Up until 1859 the SER trains did not go directly into Reading station but stopped short at their own station. This was, however, a minor and short-lived inconvenience. In 1859 a new station was built but burnt down within twelve months, after which the two lines were amalgamated into one.

The line from Wokingham to Staines was developed by the Staines, Wokingham and Woking Junction Railway (SW&WJR) in 1856. These trains were operated by the London and South Western Railway (LSWR) and offered a direct link from Wokingham to Waterloo, London.

While it is easy to scoff at the advice given to 'adventuresome' Victorian passengers about how to reduce the risks associated with train travel, which was to sit with their back to the engine and in the middle of the carriages, there is some logic and sense to this. Train journeys and trains, in general, were dangerous. This was 'modern technology', likely to malfunction and liable to explode or derail. The railway had been subject to rapid expansion, and partly as a result there was a laxness about health and safety that would not be corrected until after several major disasters, one of which was close to home.

On 12 September 1855, there was a fatal head-on crash about a mile or so outside Wokingham station. The Guildford train out of Reading was travelling at speed on the same track as the London to Reading train:

DREADFUL COLLISION ON THE READING AND REIGATE (SOUTH EASTERN) RAILWAY. FOUR PERSONS KILLED, AND SEVEN SERIOUSLY INJURED. It is with feelings of deep regret, in which, as we know all our readers will participate, that we record the most disastrous railway accident ever experienced within the limits of this neighbourhood.

Berkshire Chronicle, *15 September 1855*

There had been recent workings on the construction of the new station, which had led to all trains temporarily being placed onto the downline as a single track. On this day, a special excursion train to Brighton had been split to accommodate more people and a second driver called out for the 'new' train. This meant that there was one driver short on the Guildford train. After some running around, a replacement driver was found and, to avoid delaying the train, he jumped in the cab, fired up and set off.

An early Rolls-Royce is parked in front of Howard & Co. Garage on Broad Street in about 1906.

Meanwhile, the signals at Reading were being manned by a station porter doing a part-time job.

The net result was that four people including the driver were killed and seven were severely injured, three dying later. This was not the only rail tragedy to hit the town. There were two accidents at the level crossing, and a fatality in 1886 prompted the building of the footbridge made from railway sleepers and rails that remains to this day.

Given the current development of the new estates to the west of Wokingham, it is interesting to note that there was an abandoned plan to build a line towards Basingstoke in 1885. This would have been around 14 miles long and cut across Barkham Road just by St James's Church and Brook Farm, around the back of Barkham Square and then out across Park Lane. The proposal was never presented to the government as it was thwarted by the influence of the local hunting community and in particular of the Garth Hunt, who felt it would spoil their sport.

Much of the profit for the railways came in the early days from goods transportation; it was not until 1883 that rail companies were encouraged by government action to offer low fares, which resulted in the growth in passenger numbers such that this part of the industry started to show a return. The number of trains increased significantly to 44 per day, including the following:

6.27 LSWR – Train to Reading from Ascot and Sunninghill
7.20 LSWR – Train to Staines and London Waterloo
7.30 SER – Train to Red Hill Junction and Charing Cross
8.06 SER – Train to Reading from Charing Cross and Red Hill
Bradshaw's Railway Timetable for Wokingham, *December 1896*

The railway was electrified in 1938, and this led to a significant increase in traffic. Today, there are more trains each hour than originally on a daily basis and this schedule is designed to meet the needs of the just under 2.5 million passengers who make use of the service each year.

The car has come to dominate travel in the twenty-first century. Wokingham sits between two motorways, the M4 going west to Bath and Bristol, which was opened in 1963, and the M3, which heads to Southampton and which first opened in 1971. Both of these major roads reflect to a greater or lesser extent the old turnpikes. In the town itself, the Reading Road and the London Road follow the routes of the original tracks and turnpikes into and out of the town. The Windsor Forest turnpike milestone that remains in place outside the old Post Office building proclaims 7 miles to Reading and 32 miles to London. Passengers alighting today from their train at the station will see the spire of St Paul's Church looming over the car park, a legacy of Victorian Wokingham but one that was not built until nearly five years after the first steam train huffed and puffed and deposited its nervous passengers on the platform.

Selected References

Allington, P., Dawe, P., Hoare, B., Holland, C., King, P.(ed.), Lowe, K., Lowe, L., McLaren, J., Mitchell, C., and Watts, J. (2016) *Late Victorian Wokingham*, The Wokingham Society.
Ayres, D. (1992) 'The War of the Roses'. *Wokingham Historian*, No. 5, 7–13.
Dils, J. (1985) *An Account of Early Victorian Wokingham.*
Parliament. House of Commons (1846) *Select Committee on Reading, Guildford and Reigate Railway Bill.* Evidence 1846, Group 16, Vol. 26.
Rosevear, A. (2004) A booklet on the Turnpike Roads around Reading. *Turnpike Roads in England & Wales.* Available at: http://turnpikes.org.uk/Reading%20turnpike%20roads.htm [Accessed 31 May 2019].

3

THE GRANDER HOUSES OF WOKINGHAM

A most desirable, old fashioned Freehold Residence called Montagu House [*sic*], pleasantly situated in this picturesque and favourite town in the centre of a fashionable district, within easy driving distance of Ascot and in the midst of good hunting, while there is a capital train service to London by the South–Western and Eastern lines.

Advertisement for Montague House in The Times, *20 February 1886*

The Henry Lucas Hospital at Chapel Green is the only Grade I listed building in or near to Wokingham. It was built in 1667. The elegant almshouse has remained surrounded by quiet lanes and countryside for the last three and a half centuries, but this is likely to change as the town expands. It is about a twenty-minute walk from the town centre, from the town hall, down Denmark Street, beside Langborough Common, down Gypsy Lane and then along the Ludgrove path to the hospital; this is a walk that many incumbents at the hospital must have travelled over the centuries. The architect of the hospital was probably Sir Christopher Wren, who Henry Lucas met on several occasions together with Wren's father and uncle.

There are, amazingly, 170 Grade II★/II buildings in Wokingham.★ In Rose Street, there are thirty-three listed properties. Number 96 on the corner of

---

★ Grade I buildings are of exceptional interest. Grade II★ buildings are particularly important buildings; and Grade II buildings are of special interest.

This is probably the oldest photograph of the town, dating from about 1855, showing Shute End and The Terrace, taken before the clock tower was built. The pub sign for The Queen's Head is just visible on the right-hand side.

Wiltshire Road, The Cottage/Tudor Corner vies with No. 15 The Terrace for being the oldest in town, both dating from the fourteenth century. Many believe that No. 20 Rose Street, the WADE Centre building, is older than its sixteenth-century listing suggests. All Saints Church is also late fourteenth century, with a tower and clerestory added in the fifteenth century, but it is believed to stand on the site of a much earlier Saxon chapel.

There are many other buildings in Rose Street and around the town that date back to the fifteenth century. Indeed, seventeen listed houses date from the fifteenth century and forty-four date from the sixteenth. To put that in perspective, this is the period of the Battle of Agincourt, of the Spanish Armada, Henry VIII and Elizabeth I. Wokingham has lived through the greatest of times.

The ghosts of the past might haunt the streets of the present-day town, and if they did decide to take a nocturnal walk about Wokingham, then they would still find their way around. Even though most of the buildings have been profoundly altered during the intervening centuries and the external appearance of the houses has changed, the street layout has remained to all intents unchanged.

There are several Wealden hall houses in the town, which is a medieval timber-framed building. One example is the Hope and Anchor pub in Station Road. The original fifteenth-century building had four bays, the central two of which were connected to form a large room or hall with a hearth in the middle and an open skylight. The two end bays had second floors that jutted out into the street below.

There are attractive examples of Regency and Georgian facades, reminiscent of a child's doll's house, such as Gotelee House in Market Place and Shute End House. There are also Victorian terraces and workmen's cottages with their elegant brickwork and functional design.

Over time, various affluent or titled people have chosen to live in the town, despite its often rough and impoverished nature. They also decided to invest their money in larger or grander houses. There is Glebelands, a large country house in a parkland setting, built in 1897 by Sir Ernest Newton for the London banker Arthur Nicholson. Chetwode on Rances Lane boasted ten bedrooms with 'Capital Hunting and Good Society' when it was advertised for sale in 1897. There is No. 7 South Drive, originally known as 'Clun', a lovely house built in 1909, and designed by the architect Frank Morris whose father, Joseph, designed the police station in 1904.

There is a rich diversity of architecture around the town. Nevertheless, there are six properties in Wokingham that seem to encapsulate and reflect its history in unique ways. These seminal buildings include the town hall, which harks back to the foundation of the town and a novel form of governance; The Holt, with the now lost Beeches Manor, shares an association with the brewery trade that remains visible today; the site of Montague House has nearly 500 years of connection to education; and finally, the elegant Elms with its association with the spoils of Empire.

The Town Hall

The mock Gothic architecture of the present town hall, standing as it does amid a newly refurbished Market Place, is a spectacular but often undervalued centrepiece to the town. It dominates the town square with a Victorian characterisation that some people love, but others dislike. Irrespective of the merits of its design, the building reflects the town's long and varied history, while at the same time being a key element in the story itself.

The old town hall hosted the business of the town for many generations before it was demolished in 1858 to make way for the current building.

Like many buildings in Wokingham, the present building stands on the site of a much earlier establishment but to understand the uniqueness of the town hall it is necessary to understand the local government of medieval and Elizabethan Wokingham.

Wokingham became recognised as a town by way of a thirteenth-century market charter. Towns typically have town councils and mayors. However, Wokingham did not have this form of local government until 1885.

Until then, Wokingham's chief officer was an alderman who was elected on an annual basis and 'hath the government orderinge and direction of the said Towne and of the inhabitants thereof and of cause and matters happenynge within the Towne' as laid down in the charter of 1583 granted by Elizabeth I.

According to that charter, the Steward of Salisbury appointed the alderman from a choice of three candidates at Easter and this had been the case as long as 'the memories of men'. Indeed, it is difficult to say when the post was first created, but the word alderman is derived etymologically from the Anglo-Saxon word *ealdorman*. This term is also the source of the title earl and can be interpreted as 'elder man'. The *ealdorman* was a Saxon official who governed a shire, and so, while documentary evidence points to Wokingham's first alderman being officially appointed around 1451, the term itself stretches back before the Norman invasion.

The Wokingham alderman was not a counterpart to a powerful *ealdorman* who governed on behalf of the king. In the main, the alderman was responsible for administering the town on behalf of the Steward of the Manor of Sonning. This task meant collecting the rents of the burgage plots, looking after the weekly market and the annual fairs, as well as administering a court and collecting fines. To do this, local officials needed somewhere to meet and work.

The 1583 charter describes the first location as 'our (one) house in the Market Place called the Clockhouse' and referred to a building used by the collector of tolls. It is possible that this was the old King's Head pub, which stood next to the Red Lion until it was demolished in 1979. The King's Head became an alehouse in the mid-sixteenth century, so an early incarnation, with large rooms, could have served as the meeting place for the town council.

According to Common Council minutes, in 1680 a £5 subscription was laid on the alderman and then a duty on the burgesses to pay for repairs to the town hall, which was referred to as the 'Market House'.

In 1697, the thatched roof, no doubt a severe fire hazard in the town, was replaced with tiles. The unfortunate alderman and his officers yet again met these costs, an expense that no doubt they did not look upon willingly. Moreover, this was a cost that would become a perennial worry and headache.

Matters seem to have come to a head by 1763, when the seemingly impoverished Corporation was looking at innovative ways to fund the maintenance of the hall. They turned to a local businessman for help; his name was William Wheatley, and he was the landlord of the nearby Bush Inn.

The arrangement was that Wheatley would pay for the upkeep and repairs of the building in return for paying a nominal rent, 5*s* per year, to lease the rooms. Advertisements subsequently appeared in the *Reading Mercury* during the next couple of decades announcing balls, dances and other entertainments that Wheatley would put on, no doubt when the council were not sitting.

Wheatley seems to have set a precedent for social events at the town hall. Even after these singular arrangements had faded away, in the 1790s, dances

The delivery of a steam fire engine to the volunteer fire brigade in April 1891.
The two horses are 'tilling greys' and were called Dolly and Dustpan.

were regularly held in the building. Over time, there was a shift in focus such
that in the nineteenth century local worthier societies and groups such as
the Literary, Scientific and Mechanics Institute would meet there.

The old town hall maintained its role in Wokingham society through to the
middle of the nineteenth century, but by then the centuries-old building was
getting beyond reasonable repair. At the same time, Wokingham saw an influx
of wealthier inhabitants and the coming of the railways, which all suggested
that the town's governing body needed a more suitable building. So, in 1858,
the old town hall was demolished to make way for the new building.

Poulton and Woodman designed the new or current town hall with more
than a nod to the then-fashionable Gothic Revival style. The architects
seem to have followed the contours of the Market Place in their layout
of the building, which has an odd scarcely symmetrical footprint. Despite
all their design indulgences, the council were nevertheless very practically
minded. The old town hall had included a 'lock-up' for vagrants and offenders. It therefore seemed a sensible course of action when the new building
was being considered for the once again cash-strapped council to obtain a
contribution from the police commission. Sure enough, the new town hall
coincided with, and incorporated, the opening of the county police station
in 1860, whose sign can still be seen on the north-west side of the building.

There was a magistrates' court held in the building, and the courtyard itself was originally open to the elements and only roofed in the 1970s. Moreover, to go one better, the arches of the building housed the local fire brigade and their engines, which were initially horse-drawn and then motorised.

Many diverse groups make use of the town hall today. Local societies such as the Women's Institute hold their meetings on the first floor. There are cafés and restaurants in the courtyard where once the fire engines were parked. It houses the mayor's parlour, where the robes and chains are stored. Meetings still take place in the council chamber. The building hosts a mixture of town government, administration and social gatherings.

The Holt, Beeches Manor and the Malthouse

The Holt is nowadays the administration block for The Holt School. It is on the list of notable buildings partly because it remains a vital presence in the area but also because in the past it was the dower house of the substantial Beeches Manor.★

The manor house itself burnt down in 1961 after it had been converted to the Beeches Manor Hotel. It had stood pretty much on the site where a care home was subsequently located.

Beeches was one of several manor houses in the surrounding area, Buckhurst (St Anne's Manor) dating from around 1488, Ashridge Manor dating to 1281, Evendons mentioned in 1316, and the Norreys Manor documented in 1443.

The name Beeches derives from the de la Beche family. Roger de la Beche rented meadows from the Bishop of Salisbury, for which he paid 47*s* per annum. A corruption of Beche is thought to be the origin of Peach Street, more likely perhaps than the alternative speculation of an association with fishing or a fisherman, *le Pecheur*.

Roger died in 1294 and there was an enquiry to recognise his heir, Geoffrey. The estate that Geoffrey would inherit was sizeable and included 500 acres, a mill and ten orchards. Geoffrey atte Beche was, therefore, a wealthy man and, in 1327, he was assessed for the largest taxable sum among the residents of Wokingham.

★   A dower house is where the widow of the former lord of the manor lived.

In 1453 or 1454, a descendant of Geoffrey, Agnes de la Beche, married a local gentleman named John Whitlocke, and the manor moved into the hands of the Whitlocke family for the next few generations. The Whitlockes were lawyers and Parliamentarians, which gives some credence to a story that Cromwellian troops occupied Beeches Manor during the Civil War.

By 1683 the estate had passed to Richard Whitlocke. Richard entered into a series of financial arrangements with Richard Hawe, a brewer from Richmond. Whatever intentions Richard Whitlocke had for the money he borrowed, things did not seem to go according to plan as less than five years later, in 1687, the properties were sold to Hawe. From this point forward, there is a frequent association between the Beeches Manor house and brewing, which remains evident to this day.

Hawe seems to have been wealthy, speculative and part of a successful family. He had purchased the Norreys estate as early as 1674, from Frances, widow of Francis Peacock, who had died in 1669; Frances needed to clear the estate debts. A relative, Thomas Hawe, had leased part of the Ashridge lands in 1655 and then bought them in 1664. In his will of 1703, Thomas left the property to the son and heir of his brother, Richard Hawe. John Baldwin sold the area known as Pound Close, around what is now Station Road and Wellington Road, in 1649 to Robert Hawe, another family member; Robert transferred the land and properties to Richard in 1707.

By this stage, one man, Richard Hawe, owned an estate, a consolidation of multiple properties that covered much of Wokingham as we know it today.

In 1707, Richard Hawe let the Beeches, his brewhouse and the Bell, an inn in the town, to William Yelldall. It is the brewhouse or malthouse that remains today, on the Reading Road, and is now serving as the Masonic hall.

In 1762, the Webb family moved into the property. They were also brewers and rented the Beeches for the next fifty years.

Richard died in 1727 without children. He left the estate to his wife, Sarah, for her lifetime. When Sarah died, it passed to his six nieces, the daughters of his sister Alice Marsh. Over the next century or so, as the sisters died or relinquished their claims, the estate passed through a convoluted series of inheritances into the hands of the Crutchley and Lamplow families. These families were among the 'good and the great' of Wokingham; William Lamplow also owned Littlecourt, the future home of WADE.

The next significant occupant of the Beeches was James Haywood. In 1841, James was living at Shute End, but ten years later he was renting the

Beeches with his sister Jane. The 1851 census shows that James continued the tradition as he listed his occupation as brewer. James had very successfully taken over much of Webb's business. In fact, at one time he could boast of owning and supplying virtually all the pubs in Wokingham as well as others outside the town, such as the Leathern Bottle on the Barkham Road.

After the Haywoods moved out, other well-to-do families lived at the house. In 1876, the St Paul's church fete was held at the Beeches by permission of Mr H. Pearson, who was renting the property at the time. Then, in 1929, in 'ideal weather, the eighth annual parochial fete of St Paul's Church' was held in the grounds, this time by permission of Mr and Mrs W.H. Pountney.

However, by the 1900s, financial pressures started to force the sale of the various parts of the estate. The Norreys estate was sold off and in due course became Norreys housing estate. The Beeches was sold to a banker called France and then later in the century converted to a hotel. Sadly, the Beeches Manor Hotel was destroyed by fire on 26 June 1961. The building was empty at the time and had been scheduled for preservation because of historical interest; Wokingham had lost a vital link to its past.

The Holt, however, had been treated separately. The Humfrey family had rented the house for many years from around 1760. The Heelas family, owners of the eponymous Wokingham and Reading department stores, then became tenants in 1855. They subsequently bought it from one of the Crutchleys in 1885 and made significant alterations and modifications to the building. In 1930 the Heelas family sold The Holt to Berkshire County Council. It became a school in 1931.

Montague House

There were two Henry Mountagues, father and son, both were teachers. The family were respected and well established in the network of gentlefolk in and around Wokingham.

Henry the younger took over the running of the school around 1635. In a codicil dated 3 April 1695 Henry bequeathed:

to my son Ephraim Mountague that house tenement or messuage now in the tenancy or occupation of Richard Wethercliffe gardener and situated lying in High or Broad street of the town Oakingham in the County of Berks with all the gardens orchards stables barns and out houses.

This provides a location for the house but also indicates that the family had moved to live elsewhere in the town and that the school was no longer active.

The Mountagues' original house appears to have been cleared away completely to make way for the current building, which dates from the eighteenth and not the seventeenth century. No vestiges of an Elizabethan building have been found.

There is an engraving of the building from 1739 that shows 'The Seat of the honourable Collonel [*sic*] Williamson' in Wokingham. The picture by James Smith cleverly shows an elevated view of the house, a technique Smith used to wonderful effect, and the house as it exists today is recognisable as well as the walls to the supermarket car park. There are fields to the left and right of the house. The front garden is slightly larger than today, extending into the main concourse of Broad Street, and the back garden is laid out formally. The Oriental plane tree, which continues to grow at the edge of the supermarket car park, is not visible in this picture. This is estimated to be around 250 years old, which would suggest a planting of around 1750 and as such the tree had yet to make its arrival when the colonel lived there. Colonel Williamson, who became a lieutenant general, was the Deputy Lieutenant of the Tower of London, where he lived for several years but frequently retired to his country property. He died in 1747 and is buried in the family vault in Binfield Church.

Sometime in the eighteenth century the building acquired its Montague House appellation. A fresh association for the site with education was established with the opening of Mrs Bloom's school for 'young ladies'. There are advertisements in the *Reading Mercury* in 1792 and again in 1793 advising pupils and staff of the reopening of the school after the summer recess. Mrs Bloom rented the house through to 1801, when it was taken over by John Roberts, a wealthy solicitor and alderman. Even though Roberts significantly upgraded the house, when it came to be sold it seems to have struggled to find a buyer as it needed to be advertised in the *Reading Mercury* for an extended period from 28 November 1885 to 17 April 1886. There was even an advertisement in the prestigious *London Times* on 20 February:

The Seat of the Hon.ble Collonel Williamson in Oakingham BERKS —

Externally, Montague House appears to have hardly changed since 1739, although the gardens and surrounding countryside have disappeared under car parks and houses.

> The house admirably adapted for private or professional occupation is approached by a sweeping drive, contains 13 bedrooms, four large reception rooms, convenient offices and cellarage; stabling for three horses, yard, productive kitchen garden, divided charmingly-planted grounds with lawn, in all covering about an acre.

The house was eventually bought by local businessman Isiah Gadd, who owned several enterprises in the town including a house removals and repository business. Gadd rented the house; his tenants included Lady Catherine Eustace, and then in 1918 Gadd's daughter sold it to Lady Lydia Blain.

During the First World War, the house was used as a Forces' Club House, but soon after it became a school again when Miss Laura Baker moved her pupils in from Tudor House, on the corner of Broad Street. Grosvenor House School operated from Montague House until Miss Baker retired in the 1930s, fter which the school moved out of town, first to Albert Road, off Wellington Road, and then along Finchampstead Road to the White House; in recent years it has become Evendons Primary School. After Miss Baker left, Montague House was bought by Basil Readman, a master at nearby Wellington College.

By 1950 the house had been sold again, this time being bought by Berkshire Council, and for many years it continued to fulfil an educational purpose as the local library and adult education centre.

The Elms

Despite its exquisite Georgian exterior, The Elms can be dated back to the sixteenth century or earlier. The Grade II★ house was significantly rebuilt in the late eighteenth century, when the original timber-framed building was all but obscured. It was then extended in the 1850s and suffered a fire in 2011. Having said that, The Elms has sat on one side of Broad Street, facing Montague House on the other, for the last 300 years.

The earliest record of the house identifies it as the dower house of Swallowfield Park. Thomas Pitt bought the Swallowfield estate including The Elms in 1719. Pitt had been Governor of Bengal, India, and had made his money in Far Eastern trade; his greatest 'deal' was the Pitt or Regent Diamond, weighing 400 carats. Pitt had bought the diamond for £24,000 in 1701 and sold it to the French government in 1717 for £130,000. It was an incredible profit and a staggering amount of money, around £20 million in current values. The gem ended up on the hilt of the Emperor Napoleon's coronation sword in 1807.

During the eighteenth century, Swallowfield and The Elms were sold and resold. Pitt sold the estate for £20,770, in 1737. Nearly fifty years later, Colonel John Dodd sold it to Sylvanus Bevan, who in turn sold the estate in 1788, to Timothy Hare Earle. His son, Timothy Hare Altabon Earle, inherited Swallowfield in 1816. Pitt had made his fortune alongside the East India Company, Earle on the other had made his money in the Caribbean with sugar plantations. However, as the West Indian investments started to fail and his expensive lifestyle took its toll, Earle sold Swallowfield Park and he moved to the dower house, namely The Elms. He died there, unmarried, in 1836.

The Earles continued to own the house for the next few decades but let it to John Wheeler, a prominent local solicitor, whose wife Ellen Maria was the aunt to Jane Hayward who lived up the road at The Beeches with her brother, James. The two women were close friends, and daily visits between the two grand houses on either side of Broad Street would take place.

The 1881 census shows that Timothy Earle's widow, Anne, was living there with a footman, lady's maid, cook and laundry maid. The house was fulfilling its original purpose as a dower house. However, by 1892 the house had been sold to T.E. Ellison, who also acquired 'all the meadows and pasture land adjoining the garden and ground' from William Earle Biscoe, then owner of the Swallowfield estate.

Thomas Ellison was another Victorian gentleman who had made his money in the then British Empire; the source of his fortune was in Bengal, India. He did not marry but lived at The Elms with his mother and four unmarried sisters. Ellison was a great supporter of many local causes. After he died, his sisters continued the family's charitable involvement of the local community. Among many other charitable activities, the sisters for many years, from 1920 to 1952, allowed the town carnival to take place in the gardens of The Elms, hence the name Carnival Pool.

The last of the sisters died in 1952 and the house was sold by auction, since which time it has served as retail premises and offices and now is returning to use as luxury apartments. A few years later, in 1956, after some haggling, the then borough council bought the grounds 'for the purposes of a public open space'.

The history of each one of the 171 listed buildings warrants understanding and appreciation. Each one has its own story to tell and each narrative links Wokingham to a long and interesting legacy that reflects and is tied up with the history of England.

Selected References

Ayres, D. (1998) 'The Old Town Hall'. *The Historian*, Vol. 10, 12–24.

British Listed Buildings. Available at: https://britishlistedbuildings. co.uk/101118050-the-courtyard-wokingham#.XPFgOy3Mz1s [Accessed 31 May 2019].

Historic England *The National Heritage List for England (NHLE).* Available at: https://historicengland.org.uk/listing/the-list [Accessed 2 June 2019].

Hoare, B. (2013) *The Elms and the Ellison Family.*

Lea, R. (1994) 'The Holt Estate and Its Owners (part 1)'. *The Historian*, Vol. 7, 22–31.

Lea, J., and Lea, R. (1994) 'The Holt Estate and Its Owners (part 2)'. *The Historian*, Vol. 8, 25–34.

Must, P. (2019) *Montague House and the Mountagues.*

4

CRIME AND PUNISHMENT

WOKINGHAM COUNTY BENCH. Thomas James, labourer, was charged with assaulting P.C. Wheeler, Binfield, on the thirteenth inst. The defendant admitted pushing the constable, and the Magistrate cautioned him and discharged him … Thomas Wiggins, of 12, Albert-road, Reading, was charged with unlawfully playing cards on the G.W.R. Line, at Earley, on the 15th (Sunday)…Noah Wheatley, a tramp, was charged with being drunk in the Wokingham Road, at Earley, on the previous night. He pleaded guilty and was fined.

Reading Mercury, *Saturday, 21 June 1884*

The above reflects much of the crime that took place in and around Wokingham in the Victorian period. The town has never been a hotbed of crime in any sense, although it has suffered from the normal unlawful and antisocial behaviour that often plagues it and many similar towns today. There were also more serious crimes such as larceny, stabbings, and murders, but overall, most Wokingham citizens have lived honest, law-abiding lives. There have been, however, exceptions that have significantly and seriously carved themselves into the town's history.

A romanticised view of the highwayman Claude Duval and his 'victim' dancing a coranto.

Claude Duval

Most people have heard of Dick Turpin, the highwayman. The romanticised stories of his boldness and cunning have been played out in many stories and films. Turpin had been born in Whitechapel; he lived and 'worked' as a highwayman, in and around Epping Forest. However, few people are aware that Wokingham harboured its own highwayman, Claude Duval, who set the standard of gallantry to which others needed to aspire.

Duval was of French descent, from a noble family whose reduced circumstances necessitated that he be sent to Paris from Normandy to work as a servant. Duval found suitable employment with exiled British Royalists who had fled England during the Civil War. Sometime around 1660, after the Restoration of Charles II, Duval decided that he would come to England in attendance on the Duke of Richmond. He soon left the duke and moved to Wokingham, renting a house somewhere in the town. It was here, for want of a more respectable career, that Duval took to highway robbery across Bagshot Heath and into Swinley Forest.

Duval's approach to his new profession was to avoid the use of violence and act in a gentlemanly manner, wearing fashionable clothes. The pinnacle of his exploits was when he stopped a coach in which a gentleman and his wife were travelling with £400 in cash, which was equivalent to a staggering £45,000 today. The lady, for whatever reason, decided it was an opportune moment to play the flageolet, a small wind instrument related to the recorder. Duval responded by asking the lady to dance with him on the roadside. His request was granted, and a coranto dance was performed while the husband watched. The audience, namely the husband, was then asked to pay for his entertainment.

This gallantry, much as it gathered admirers around him, did not mask the underlying criminal nature of Duval's actions and he was eventually caught and sentenced at the Old Bailey. Despite pleas from his devoted following, he was hanged at Tyburn on 21 January 1670. His body was cut down and effectively 'laid in state' at Tangier Tavern, St Giles, where the crowds that came to visit were so large that they needed to be curtailed by court order. The end of the story, as tradition would have it, is that he was subsequently laid to rest in St Paul's, Covent Garden, where his memorial can be read today:

> Here lies DuVall: Reder, if male thou art,
> Look to thy purse; if female, to thy heart.
> Much havoc has he made of both; for all
> Men he made to stand, and women he made to fall
> The second Conqueror of the Norman race,
> Knights to his arm did yield, and ladies to his face.
> Old Tyburn's glory; England's illustrious Thief,
> DuVall, the ladies' joy; DuVall, the ladies' grief.

The Blacks

The South Sea Company had been established to encourage people to invest in the much-anticipated rewards coming from the discovery of the glamorous South Seas. This was considered a viable strategy for reducing the national debt. The stock attracted increasing numbers of investors as its value rose, but its worth was based more on hype rather than the reality of the riches to be gathered by exploiting the natural resources of South America.

When the 'bubble' burst and the share price collapsed, many were left broke, bankrupt or just less well off.

Wokingham was not isolated from the economic downturn that followed the collapse in 1720. The loss of their investments put pressures on the hitherto wealthy and affluent and led to a general tightening of purse strings all round.

In Windsor Forest, this austerity was associated with an increase in land enclosures and a toughening of the already burdensome forest laws that limited, among other things, who could and could not hunt or shoot in the forest. Local farmers and businessmen were taken to the local forest courts for hunting deer or birds from their own lands, while at the same time fashionable parties were coming down from London composed of the well-heeled and well-connected.

In response to the social and economic tensions created by the South Sea bubble, a group of Wokingham men decided that some form of direct action was needed. Initially, the gang set out as poachers of the 'Royal' deer and yet to categorise them merely as common criminals is probably misreading the situation. While many described them as ruffians and thugs, they were also representatives of a class of professionals and tradespeople that would morph over the centuries into the middle class.

The leader of the gang was William Shorter of Wokingham, a local farmer. Other members were:

* Edward Collier, a felt maker of Wokingham
* George Wynne, a clockmaker of Wokingham
* Richard Fellows, a butcher of Maidenhead
* Edward Stevens, a farrier of Easthampstead
* James Barlow, an innkeeper of Winkfield
* Charles Rackett, of Bagshot, a gentleman and brother-in-law
  of Alexander Pope
* John Perryman of Oakley Green, a gentleman

They put soot on their face or 'blacked up' to avoid identification. The Wokingham Blacks followed on from the activities of the Waltham Blacks, of Hampshire, who supposedly modelled themselves on Robin Hood.

The actions of the Blacks were deliberate and well planned. The Wokingham Blacks started by targeting Earl Cadogan's estate at Caversham, but they also sought retribution on those they considered had behaved unfairly to the general population. For instance, a Dr Smith had ordered some hay from a local man, which, when it was delivered, had been spoilt; the doctor refused to pay until the Blacks threatened him with pistols and a blunderbuss.

The Waltham Blacks stepped over the line when they directed their antagonism towards the Prince of Wales. They intercepted a consignment of wine destined for the prince and told the 'conductors' that they 'now had got wherewith to make a Festival and drink his Health'.

The Blacks had accused a Easthampstead clergyman called Thomas Power of treason and he had, in turn, accused the Blacks of assault. Power was, in fact, an agent provocateur and, when two men came from London to seek out the truth, the Blacks stepped forward to give information. They were arrested, taken to London and interrogated.

William Shorter escaped by literally breaking out of the room in which he was being held. Wynne and Collier were not so lucky, and other members of the gang were rounded up, including John Hawthorne, who had been accused of the murder of an innkeeper's son in Old Windsor.

These were therefore seen as political as well criminal acts, and subsequently, the underlying class conflicts became reflected in the harshness of the punishments and the subsequent response from the government.

The Black Act was passed in May 1723 and specified that anyone who blackened or disguised themselves or was an accessory after the fact or who was found in or near a forest or Royal Park could be sentenced to death. The Act created a further fifty crimes including fishing, the hunting of hares, the destruction of trees and any form of hunt sabotage where the death penalty could be enforced.

It has been called the most draconian of English laws and remained on the statute books for 100 years.

As the members of the Blacks were rounded up, they were tried and sentenced. In June four were hanged for murder, and six transported for stealing deer. This was effectively the end for the Wokingham Blacks. The Waltham Blacks did carry out further raids over the next couple of months, but the offenders were caught, and the full force of the Act was brought to bear.

However, for the Wokingham Blacks, the picture was not completely grim. Thomas Wynne, the local clockmaker, was subsequently released on the grounds of his being of 'creditable reputation'.

Edward Collier, who had been sentenced to seven years' transportation to America for stealing a deer from Sir Robert Rich, escaped prison and went into hiding in Windsor Forest. On Sir Robert's death, Collier gave himself up and fell on the mercy of Sir Robert's widow. The widow relented, and he was pardoned. In 1730 Edward's wife gave birth to twins who were baptised at All Saints, Wokingham, on 30 September 1730.

As for William Shorter, he was never caught and simply disappeared into the landscape.

The 'Swing' Riots

Policing and law enforcement were local matters that were the responsibility of the town justices and council. There had been a Wokingham Association for the Prosecution of Felons as early as 1775, which met at the King's Head pub to arrange for the apprehension of offenders and deal out their punishments. In the 1830s, there was a special Forest Association for the Prosecution of Felons, which met regularly at The Roebuck to deal with a specific threat to both life and property; this was the 'Swing' Riots.

There had been poor harvests in Berkshire in 1829 and 1830. Farmers and landowners had responded by investing in the newer technology of the agricultural revolution such as the horse-powered threshing machine; they had also reduced wages. All of this put pressure on traditional agricultural workers, who saw their livelihoods and indeed their way of living under threat. Their response was to organise themselves and fight back. Their tactics were to cause disruption by burning ricks and destroying machinery. These were called the machine or Swing Riots after the mythical leader Captain Swing, whose name was signed on the threatening letters sent to magistrates and farmers.

In response, the local farmers and other notables formed voluntary associations to combat the wave of anticipated trouble. The Forest Association was created in 1832 and appointed 102 special constables in Wokingham, and roughly the same number around the district. Their job was to detect and apprehend likely offenders and to deal with any crimes that took place.

Early in the troubles, a hayrick was set alight at Green's farm in Barkham. The following year, on 15 January 1833, there was another fire at a farm in King Street.

The minutes from the Forest Association meetings provide a revealing insight into the events that took place. The Forest Association picked up

Punishments for comitting crimes were harsh and often involved public humiliation. The town stocks were located on the left of the covered ground floor of the old town hall.

the 'bar bill' at the Bull at Barkham and the Rose in Wokingham in recompense for services rendered by the 'officers' in dealing with the fire in Barkham. The bill for refreshments at the Pheasant on King Street was also paid during the night when George Ellis, 'a suspicious character', was apprehended. A Wokingham woman called Sarah Keep was paid 10s for providing information that led to the arrest of a perpetrator and troublemaker. In total there were 165 incidents recorded around Berkshire, many in the west of the county and mainly around Newbury. However, the preventative measures and swift responses of the Forest Association seem to have had their effect and quelled further political unrest such that, after the initial spate of incidents, there appear to have been few criminal acts afterwards in the neighbourhood of Wokingham.

The Police

The Wokingham Association represented the type of local initiative and organisation that was the primary approach to keeping the peace until 1856, when the Country and Borough Police Act required the establishment of a local police force.

The Police Act prompted the establishment of the new police force in Wokingham, and by 1860 it had moved into its home, namely the newly opened town hall. The legend 'County Police Station' can be seen on the west wall of the building. The entrance was on the north side and included an office, kitchen, four cells and stables; there were seven bedrooms on the first floor. The police also took on the role of fire brigade until 1876, when the local Wokingham Volunteer Fire Brigade was established.

Petty sessions were held at the town hall every Tuesday morning but, judging by the reports in the *Reading Mercury* for the later part of the century, Wokingham was not a hive of crime. There was a spate of burglaries in the 1870s, the theft of thirteen young ducks from the roadside in Woodley and the fine of 14*s* 6*d* including costs against one Thomas Goswell of Wokingham, carpenter, for allowing his donkey to stray upon the highway. Petty crimes in the main, but interspersed with murder, drunkenness and domestic violence.

By the start of the twentieth century, the town hall had become cramped and a new purpose-built building was opened on the corner of Rectory and Milton Roads. It was designed by Joseph Morris and contained five cells, a magistrates' court, and charge room, as well as accommodation for four single constables and two married constables and a sergeant. It ceased to be an active police station around the turn of the millennium, although the magistrates' court had closed earlier; it became a listed building in 1987.

Superintendent Charles Goddard was in charge at Wokingham from 1903 until his retirement in 1933, and an insight into his style of policing is revealed by this recollection:

> Superintendent Goddard was very keen on drill. Many can still recall with pride the days when stationed at Wokingham, they formed part of a line of men paraded across the road and then doubled to the Town Hall to surround that edifice with all possible speed. This drill proved to the Superintendent that his men could be dispatched to a given point in the shortest possible time or deal with truculent mobs.

Today, policing in Wokingham is part of the Thames Valley beat and although the town has grown significantly since the days of Superintendent Goddard

The town hall housed the fire brigade engines, both horse-drawn and motorised, for many years.

Wokingham were divisional winners of the 1904 Berkshire Constabulary tug of war challenge.

the level of crime remains relatively low. Having said that, Wokingham has sadly witnessed some high-profile cases.

Armed Raid at Arborfield REME

In 1955, the quiet of the local countryside was disturbed by a robbery by the IRA at the Hazebrouck Barracks.

Early in the morning of 13 August a man wearing the battle dress of the 5th Training Battalion approached the sentry. The guard and the sergeant in charge found themselves confronted with a pistol and were bound and gagged. The man was joined by twelve other men, who quickly rounded up the guards in the main guardroom and forced them into cells. The four sentries who were outside were similarly overpowered. None of the sixteen soldiers had been armed. The attackers turned their attention to the armoury and stole weapons and ammunition, including a light machine gun and pistols. By 3.30 in the morning the raiders were on their way with their haul in vans and cars. It was an hour and a half later that the sergeant was able to free himself and raise the alarm.

The area was put on lockdown with police roadblocks and vehicle checks. Three men were stopped and arrested in a car in Ascot. A couple of days later, on 17 August, the haul was discovered in an abandoned shop in north London.

The arrested men were charged at Wokingham magistrates' court amid intense security. Their trial subsequently took place at Reading assizes.

Murder of Mark Tildesley

The Frank Ayres Funfair arrived in town at the start of half-term week in May 1984. The funfair frequented the town roughly four times a year and was set up on Carnival Field, on the corner of Wellington and Finchampstead Roads.

Mark Tildesley, like many other children, was keen to go. He was 7 years old, lived just off Rose Street and went to Palmer Junior School (now All Saints School). He was supplementing his 30p per week pocket money by collecting trolleys at Tesco along Denmark Street and pocketing the 10p coins customers had deposited to unlock them from the rack. Late in the afternoon, Mark spent 50p on some sweets; 50p that he had been given by a man who suggested that if he came back later to the fair, he would get some free rides.

Mark went back home, had his tea, and left on his gold Raleigh bike around 6 p.m., telling his mother that he would be back by 7.30. He never returned.

Around 8 p.m. his worried parents went looking for him. They found his bike chained to some railings near the fair and reported him missing to the police. What would prove to be a fruitless search began later that evening.

Over the coming days, the police interviewed all the stallholders at the fair. Police officers made door-to-door visits to every house in town. Soldiers were called in to support the search. The then latest heat-seeking technology was used to cover fields around and about the town. All to no avail.

Mark's disappearance in a small market town became national news. There was television coverage on the BBC's *Crimewatch UK* programme, but, despite 2,500 potential leads, nothing substantive emerged.

Detective Superintendent Roger Nicklin, who was leading the investigation, conceded after two weeks of enquiries that the police had 'absolutely no idea about Mark's disappearance'. The only vague clue was that several witnesses mentioned that there was a 'stooping man' hanging around town that afternoon.

The name of a fairground worker, Sidney Cooke, came up in the police investigations. Cooke was interviewed but claimed he was at a fairground in Hendon that night; Cooke was released, but the police kept his name on file. After eighteen months and despite many efforts and attention, the investigation wound down in October 1985. It was as if little Mark Tildesley had merely vanished off the planet.

Five years later the Metropolitan Police, in London, launched an inquiry, called Operation Orchid, into the disappearance of missing children. In December 1990, the police interviewed Leslie Bailey. Bailey, who had learning disabilities, was in Wandsworth Prison for the murder of 14-year-old Jason Swift and 6-year-old Barry Lewis. When Bailey, who was known as 'Catweazle' after the TV programme character, was questioned he had on him a map and handwritten letter from a fellow inmate. The map pinpointed the location where Mark Tildesley had been murdered and had been addressed to Sidney Cooke, who was also serving a prison sentence for the murder of Jason Swift.

Bailey confessed, and the police realised that Cooke, whom his co-workers called 'Hissing Sid', was the 'stooping man'.

On that evening in June 1984, Bailey had driven Lennie Smith of the so-called Dirty Dozen Gang from Hackney to Wokingham. Cooke was hosting what they described as a party in a caravan near the fair. At Wokingham, Smith went and found Cooke in Langborough Road and together in a white Triumph 2000 they drove to Evendons Lane. In the back of the car was Mark.

In a field called The Moors, Cooke had given Tildesley a glass of milk laced with a muscle relaxant. More muscle relaxant was given in tablet form. After about an hour, it became apparent that Mark was dead. It was probably no later than 7.30 p.m.

Bailey and Smith drove back to London, leaving Cooke to dispose of the body.

In October 1991, Leslie Bailey was charged with the murder of Mark Tildesley and received two life sentences. He was murdered in prison by two fellow inmates in 1992.

Cooke was never charged with any involvement in Mark Tildesley's death, despite him being named by the judge in Bailey's case, and despite a tiger ring, identical to one owned by Mark, being found in Cooke's repossessed car in 1985.

Cooke was paroled from prison in 1998 after serving nine years for his involvement in the murder of Jason Swift. Within twelve months he was arrested again and charged by the police with eighteen offences. He received two life sentences and, at the time of writing, remains in prison. Mark's body has never been found.

Selected References

Deb, H.C. (1955) *Arms Theft, Arborfield*, Vol. 545 cc6–8. Available at: *https://api.parliament.uk/historic-hansard/written-answers/1955/oct/25/arms-theft-arborfield* [Accessed 3 June 2019].

Ford, D., *Royal Berkshire History* (online). Available from www.berkshire-history.com/bios/cduval.html Nash Ford Publishing [Accessed 24 April 2019].

Heelas, A.T. (1928) *Historical Notes on Wokingham*.

Hosking, J.R. (1989) 'Wokingham Police Station'. *The Wokingham Historian,* No. 1, 19–21.

Roger, P. (1974) 'The Waltham Blacks and the Black Act Pat Rogers'. *The Historical Journal,* Vol. 17, No. 3 (Sep.), 465–486. Published by Cambridge University Press.

Thompson, E.P. (1975) *Whigs and Hunters: The Origins of the Black Act,* Breviary Stuff Publications.

5

WELFARE AND EDUCATION

It has pleased God to allow Cholera to enter England again, and no one can say what places shall or shall not be visited by it. The Doctors tell us they can do much to prevent it but not so much to cure it. You can do very much for yourself to lessen its violence.

The Wokingham Parish Magazine, *September 1866*

Sanitation

Basic sanitation was for Wokingham, as for many towns, a severe problem in the Victorian period. In the middle of the nineteenth century, Wokingham's water supply was drawn from 280 wells scattered around the town. This water was being used for business and personal use. At the same time, there was no systematic or hygienic way to dispose of waste material; effluent flowed directly back into the watercourse. There were tanneries along the Emm Brook just out of town. There were regular cattle markets in the town itself.

In London, there was the 'Big Stink', which referred to the general foulness of the River Thames. It was so bad that Queen Victoria had to cancel a riverboat trip because of the smell and Parliament needed to move its business to St Albans. The smell was the symptom of the dire state of the sanitation or lack thereof. The poor sanitation and hygiene brought associated illness and disease. Cholera had first reached England in the port

There was serious disruption when the sewage pipes were laid in Peach Street but the need for improved sanitation was long overdue.

of Sunderland in 1831. The disease is associated with poor sanitation or unclean drinking water. It arrived in Wokingham in 1856 and then reoccurred during the next decade.

The 'Big Stink' prompted action in the capital and subsequently elsewhere throughout the country. The Public Health Act of 1848 compelled local towns to take action to remedy the situation; in some areas, this was completed more quickly than others.

By 1866, the situation in the country had generally not improved and a new law, the Sewage Utilisation Act, was needed to force local authorities to take action.

Wokingham, in 1870, while priding itself on being a healthy and pleasant place to live, had a sickness and death rate more consistent with an industrialised city than the rural market town that it was. But still the local council hesitated; concerns about the cost, the disruption and general loss of trade as the changes were undertaken in the town centre encouraged a laissez-faire attitude.

This attitude, the ongoing delay and the poor health statistics angered the local government authority, who sent in their 'special agent' Inspector John

Thornhill Harrison. His report was damning. The water was fundamentally unfit for human consumption. It was a direct cause of much illness in the town. Harrison also reported that samples he had collected represented 'the worst waters I have ever met with. It has more than twice the manure value than average London sewage'.

Nevertheless, it would take more than a decade for real improvements to be carried out. Water pipes had to be laid throughout the town, Broad Street and Peach Street were dug up, and a sewage farm was built in the triangle between the railway, Molly Millars Lane and Barkham Road. Over time, matters improved and, as Wokingham entered the twentieth century, basic sanitation was at long last in place.

The Workhouse

The image of the Dickensian workhouse is probably not too far from the truth. Workhouses were not designed to be pleasant; the strictness and harshness of the daily routine were to encourage the poor and the disadvantaged to find work and provide for themselves. This was not merely a case of 'tough love'; the civil parish bore the cost of these institutions, which meant the local inhabitants would have to pay and as such anything that would reduce this financial burden was to be welcomed. On the other side, the charitable instincts of the citizens of Wokingham ensured that support for those in need was provided.

The Wokingham workhouse is recorded as early as 1776. It could house up to fifty inmates, although for much of the time there were fewer than twenty-five. The workhouse was initially located in Denmark Street; it had a single fireplace in the kitchen, there were a few beds for the master and his family, but inmates would sleep on the floor. The inhabitants were the old, the infirm, sometimes the mentally ill, although specific institutions existed for their 'care', and unmarried mothers. In the workhouse, an inmate was forced to work, and this could mean anything from general labouring to, at one time, being engaged in the silk industry that flourished for a while in the town. Failure to complete the allocated task would lead to punishment; James Murphy, for example, was imprisoned for fourteen days for refusing to work. The borderline between the workhouse and prison was a narrow one.

The legislation covering workhouses changed in 1834 under the Poor Law Amendment Act. Rather than being the responsibility of the local parish, the Act gave the Poor Law Commission the power to unite parishes into unions, each union being administered by a local board of guardians. The Wokingham Poor Law Union was formed in 1835 and consisted of local parishes including Arborfield, Barkham, Earley as well as Shinfield, Sonning, Swallowfield, Wargrave and Winnersh.

The Wokingham Poor Law Union set up two workhouses, one in Wargrave for the northern part of the district and one in Swallowfield for the southern region. The establishment of these new institutions made the old workhouse in Denmark Street redundant, and it was closed down. The Wargrave building, however, seems to have been defective as the guardians' minute book of September 1846 found it damp and lacking in ventilation. As a result, according to the *Reading Mercury* of 29 July, 'The Guardians of the Wokingham Union propose to build a new workhouse for the accommodation of their poor, instead of sending them to Wargrave House.'

Land was purchased on the Barkham Road leading out of town and a brand new workhouse constructed for the housing of up to 200 inmates.

The following report dated June 1893 provides an insight into the level of poverty that could afflict the inhabitants of Wokingham, even toward the end of the nineteenth century:

William Haines and Charlotte Haines, his wife, were summoned for neglecting and exposing their five children, whose ages range from 11 to 3 years, at Wokingham, in a manner likely to cause them unnecessary suffering. Mr Sydney Brain, of Reading, appeared to prosecute, and in opening, the case said that it was such a bad one that amounted a public scandal. Inspector Bennett, said that on the 27th May he came to Wokingham, and saw four children belonging to the prisoners standing outside the 'Wheatsheaf'. Witness saw the female prisoner in that house. He had a conversation with her, and she arranged to fetch her husband. He waited about two hours, and he then saw the fifth child, named Kate. Witness subsequently saw Mrs Haines and the three youngest children secreted behind a hedge. He examined the children, who were in a filthy condition swarming with vermin, which on one of the children had caused sores. Witness then gave in detail the condition of the children, who were badly clothed, and a horrible smell arose from their bodies. He communicated with the police, and the male defendant was brought to P.C. Finch. Witness got the family lodgings that night. The family afterwards went to the Workhouse, where they were thoroughly cleansed. Supt. Atkin said on the thirteenth May the defendants and their family were ejected from Chubb's Row, since which date they had had no proper habitation, and they had been sleeping rough. He had had frequent complaints respecting the children. On the thirteenth ult., at 11.30 p.m., the male defendant came to witness and asked him what he could do with two children. The man was drunk, and he and his children were allowed to sleep that night in a stable at the 'Eagle'. Since then he had seen the children in the streets; they were very filthy and poorly clad. Witness communicated with Inspector Bennett. On Monday he found the three youngest children in a shed at the back of the 'Wheatsheaf', where they had been sleeping the two previous nights. The children there were apparently well fed. Witness subsequently gave instructions for the family to be taken to the Workhouse. The man, who was formerly a blacksmith, was often in public house, and, as well as his wife, was addicted to drink.

'Wokingham Petty Assizes',
Reading Mercury, *19 June 1893*

This story reveals that drunkenness, addiction, unemployment, child welfare and homelessness are not solely aspects or themes of modern-day living, but also that there were 'safety nets' in place more than 100 years ago to try and provide some welfare and care for the afflicted and less well-off inhabitants of the town.

In 1939, the Union Workhouse on the Barkham Road became an emergency hospital to cater for the wounded coming back from the war. In 1948 it was renamed Wokingham Hospital.

Schooling

Literacy in Berkshire in the eighteenth century could have been as low as 25 per cent, but over the next 150 years it would increase to all but 100 per cent. Literacy, education and upskilling went hand in glove with the needs of the economy and society.

Wokingham has benefitted from the goodwill of many benefactors who saw education as a way to lift the poorer members of society upward: spiritually, economically and socially.

Martin's School

In his will dated 4 September 1673, Thomas Martin left an annuity of £6 to be paid from his land called Fieldhurst. The money was to be used to keep five male children, for a limited period of three years, at school and to give them annually a new cloth coat and a pair of shoes. The endowment also provided for a pair of breeches. The five boys selected were to be between the age of 10 and 11 years old and should comprise three children born in the parish and two from outside.

By 1784, Martin's School had been merged with the Palmer School, and the number of children supported increased to eight. Two teachers shared responsibilities for the combined schools, John Nethercliff and Joseph Spier.

In 1828, the National School was built in Rose Street and amalgamated with Palmer and Martin's Schools.

Palmer Schools

Charles and Martha Palmer were both philanthropic and donated what was at the time a significant amount of money towards schooling in the town.

Charles Palmer was a doctor from Arborfield and in his will dated 1711 he gave to the minister of the parish church in Wokingham £10 per annum with the request that he should preach a sermon on 15 February in the morning for the encouragement of charity.

He also gave to the town and parish the yearly sum of £20. This endowment was for the upkeep and maintenance of a school for twenty poor boys; twelve boys were to come from out of the town and eight from within the parish. Charles also empowered the electors of the charity, including the alderman and the minister, to employ a diligent person to be schoolmaster, who was paid £15 per annum, for the boys and ensure that they achieve apprenticeships in mechanical trades

In this 1896 photograph children at Palmer Schools proudly display their 100 per cent attendance medals over two years.

In 1713, Martha Palmer, a spinster, donated the rent from land valued at £400 as well as £15 per annum for a schoolmistress for the education of twelve poor girls, eight of the parish and four of the town. The girls should be taught, up to the age of 12, to sew, knit and spin cloth.

Martha's charity also ensured that there were materials for the girls to work with, wood for the fire in cold weather, shoes and books. The girls were to receive a Bible with the Common Prayer Book in it as well as a book entitled *The Whole Duty of Man*, an English Protestant devotional work. The girls should refer to each other as sisters, and the school would be called The Maiden School.

When the Palmer and Maiden Schools were incorporated into the National School in 1828, Martha Palmer's endowment to provide clothing to the poor children of Wokingham continued and remained in place for many years after that.

St Paul's Parish Schools

John Walter III took over *The Times* newspaper from his father and was a major benefactor to good causes in and around Wokingham.

There is a lot in the locality that is owed to the generosity of the Walter family. Both the village school in Finchampstead and St Paul's Parish School in town owe their existence to the generosity of John Walter III; he owned *The Times* newspaper and was High Steward of Wokingham. The Parish School was opened in 1866, a couple of years after the consecration of the church, with 325 mixed children and infants. Over the years, the school expanded thanks to the generosity of John and that of his son Arthur, with the addition of a more extensive playground, parish rooms and the clock tower.

When the Walter estate was being sold off in 1911, Thomas Ellison of The Elms bought the schools as well as the parish rooms and clock tower and donated them to the parish. In return for his charity, Ellison was presented with a silver casket by the parishioners.

Over time the junior section of the Parish School moved to become St Paul's Junior C of E School in Murray Road and the infant school joined St Paul's Junior School in Oxford Road in 1979.

The National and British Schools

The Church of England was resistant in the early part of the nineteenth century to the notion of secular education. Education should, they believed, include a religious and spiritual dimension alongside the 3 Rs (reading, writing and arithmetic). The Church of England founded The National Society for Promoting the Education of the Poor in The Principles of the Established Church of England, which prompted the Anglican Church in Wokingham to set up the National School in 1825 for 250 boys and girls in Rose Street.

By way of contrast, the British Schools were established based on non–conformist, non–denominational Protestant leanings. The British School in Wokingham was founded by the Baptist Church in Milton Road for the children of 'dissenting parents whose poverty prevented them from supplying a means for their education'. It opened in 1841 for around 200 children and is now a Grade II listed building.

Miss Baker's School

Miss Laura Jane Baker came to Wokingham from Warminster as a governess in the 1880s. She must have been a very good one as very soon other parents wanted her to teach their children. As a result, Laura and her sister Lucy set up a school for seven children at The Retreat in Milton Road in 1890. Laura would do the teaching and Lucy the housekeeping.

The school quickly outgrew its premises, and in 1893 Miss Baker moved into Terrace Point, now known as Tudor House, and renamed it Grosvenor School, to which a kindergarten and dedicated library were added. By now the school boasted ten teachers and more than sixty pupils.

Miss Baker, along with other members of Wokingham's society, was a 'passive dissenter'. Education had been made compulsory for children up to the age of 10 in 1880. Up until that date, schooling had been basic and limited to the children of wealthier parents or the charitable acts of benefactors. The 1902 Education Act built upon the earlier legislation but specified the curriculum that needed to be followed. Education would be paid for by the poor rate and its spending administered through the Church (Church of England Schools). 'Passive dissenters', like Laura Baker, believed that this was tantamount to supporting a particular religious view and dogma, and that schools per se should be sectarian. She therefore held back the part of her poor rate that was to be allocated for educational purposes. As a result, she was fined more than once during the first decade of the century.

The school grew and, after a further fifteen years, needed to move again, this time to Montague House. Here Miss Baker was able to create a school to her design: there was a school hall and dining room at one end of the house and two grass tennis courts at the back, as well as a croquet lawn, a walled garden and a summer house. By then, the school was substantial and there were some 100 students including forty boarders.

When the Wokingham County Girls' School (now The Holt School for Girls) opened in 1931, most of the 11-year-olds and upwards moved from Grosvenor School and Miss Baker's continued as a day school for younger children.

Miss Baker eventually retired in 1933 and the school was taken over by her nieces, Olive and Janet Knight, daughters of Lucy. The school was now known as Wokingham Preparatory School and in 1947 moved to Albert Road. Subsequently, when numbers increased, it moved again, to the White House on the corner of Evendons Lane and Finchampstead Road. It is now Evendons Primary School.

The social care and supportive infrastructure that developed through the twenty-first century and with which we are familiar today bears witness to the progress made in helping those less fortunate and providing the right to education for all. Having said that, this progress should not detract from or diminish the charitable efforts and endeavours that provided a degree of social support in the Victorian period and earlier.

Selected References

Allington, P., Dawe, P., Hoare, B., Holland, C., King, P. (ed.), Lowe, K., Lowe, L., McLaren, J., Mitchell, C., and Watts, J. (2016) *Late Victorian Wokingham*, The Wokingham Society.

Bell, J. (2017) *Miss Baker's School and Other Wokingham Memories.*

Butchart, O. and Bell, J. (2006) *19th Century St James' Parish Magazine Extracts.*

Goswell, M. (1990) Martin's School Wokingham. *Wokingham Historian*, No. 2, 1–3.

Hoare, B. (2013) *The Elms and the Ellison Family.*

6

FOOD, BUT MAINLY DRINK!

There is no place in England more given to frequent enebrious meetings, continual drinking than they (in Windsor Forest) … for there is not a hamlet amongst them that is not furnished with three or four alehouses at the least.

Thomas Young, 1617

The Rise of the Public House

In 1580, rather than the standard three or four alehouses, there were sixteen alehouses in Wokingham with a further two inns, serving the needs of around 750 inhabitants.

The Elizabethan ale or beer houses were the natural consequence of a long medieval custom of brewing and selling any excess beer to your neighbours. The basic brewing process is relatively simple but does require dedicated equipment and know-how, so it is likely that not everyone would find the time, space or inclination needed. Over time, what can be thought of as a home-based enterprise, typically for the old, lame or widowed needing an ongoing income, became a more full-time occupation and business. The various legislations and taxes that were then applied to beer production and marketing made it more of a profession and trade.

The Queen's Head, pictured in 1906, has been selling beer since 1777.

The number of establishments in Tudor Wokingham is indicative of the important and various roles that these beer houses performed.

First of all, Wokingham had a weekly market and there was, therefore, a need to go somewhere to get something to drink and to eat.

The limited number of inns providing overnight lodging reflects the fact that Wokingham is not, nor has been, on any major highway or road. Few travellers would pass through the town, although many would visit for the market and for the two annual fairs.

Drinking beer was healthy, or at least was less dangerous than drinking the water, which typically would have been polluted. And the beer houses would be in a better position to cook food and sell it in bite-size portions. In many instances, this 'fast-food service' could be provided on credit, 'on the slate', as an early form of payday loans but one that would put additional financial pressures on the supposedly already burdened keeper.

The beer house also served as the hub of a social network where local news could be shared and information about work opportunities and items for sale could be exchanged, or simply as a place to spend some time on a chilly night.

They also provided a prominent role in the actual running of the town. Up until the eighteenth century, much of the town's administration and the meetings of the council would take place in The Roebuck or The Red Lion.

The 1830 Beer Act reduced taxes and at the same time made it easy for someone to acquire a licence to sell beer from their house (a beer house or a public house). At this time, Wokingham experienced a growth spurt, brought about by the arrival of the railway. By the end of the century, Wokingham could boast forty-one licensed premises.

A Bit of a Pub Crawl, and a Stag Night!

The story of Wokingham's pubs through the twentieth and into the twenty-first century is one of steady decline and closures. Changes in society, how and where we eat and drink, have all had their toll; having said that, the town remains blessed with some great town centre and just-out-of-town pubs.

The oldest beer houses and inns that we know about date from the early seventeenth century. The Cock, the George, the Hart, the Hinde and the Bell are all pub or inn signs that are no longer with us.

It is probably not too much to say that the spirits (no pun intended) of the town's oldest pub lives on in Bush Walk and the Rose Revived.

In 1701, a Mrs Sampson was named as the licensee of the Bush Inn, which was owned at that time by local brewer John Hawes. However, there is some indication that 'the Busshe' existed in 1562 and was owned by a Marmaduke Beake of Evendon. The Rose Revived is actually the latest iteration of three Roses.

The first Rose, adjacent to the Bush Inn, most likely started in the seventeenth century, and by 1734 was owned by Molly and Sarah Mogg. Molly is the eponymous 'Fair Maid' of the poem 'Molly Mogg, or the Fair Maid of the Inn'. The poem was written by John Gay with contributions from Alexander Pope and Dean Swift, and was first published in 1726. The poem was supposedly composed one wet afternoon when the three writers were taking shelter at the inn and deals with the unrequited love of the Edward Standen, heir to the Arborfield Estate, for the beautiful Molly. Here is a short extract:

A rather run-down Bush Hotel, probably around the 1900s. The sign above the door reads simply 'Billiards'.

Says my Uncle, I pray you discover,
What hath been the cause of your woes,
Why you pine and you whine like a lover?
I've seen Molly Mog of the Rose.

Oh, nephew, your grief is but folly,
In town you may find better prog;
Half-a-crown there will get you a Molly,
A Molly much better than Mog.

The School Boy's delight is a play day,
The School Master's joy is a flog.
The Milkmaid's delight is a May day,
But mine is on sweet Molly Mog.

John Chaplin had leased the Rose in 1752 and had built the trade successfully, including offering a post-chaise for hire service for his more moneyed clientele. For a brief time, the Rose took over from the Bush as the starting point for the Wokingham to London stagecoach but, when Chaplin lost this franchise, he became involved in the Wokingham Fly as a second stagecoach offering.

Things went awry, however, in 1772 when the lease for the no doubt profitable Rose came up for renewal and the owner John Griffin, the son-in-law of Sarah Mogg, asked for a price that Chaplin was not able or prepared to pay. As such, he moved his business along the road to the New Rose in Peach Street:

> John Chaplin at the Rose Inn returns his grateful thanks to the Nobility, Gentry & Others for the many Favours that they have confirmed upon him for upwards of twenty years at the above inn … As his lease will expire at Midsummer next … and his landlord not chusing [*sic*] to grant a fresh one without an advanced Rent & other Incumbrances, he takes the earliest opportunity to inform them, that he has purchased a HOUSE in Peake Street a few doors up from his present Inn which he is fitting in a genteel manner for their accommodation & humbly hopes for a Continuance of their Favour.
>
> Berkshire Chronicle, *17 February 1772*

The plot thickened, however, when later that same year William Wheatley took over the lease of the former or Old Rose and combined it with the Bush, as outlined in another announcement:

> Mr Wheatley has taken the Old Rose [later Molly Mogg's] … where he hopes that the deficiencies of his house the Bush (which is now joined to the Rose) will be amply made amends for.
>
> Berkshire Chronicle, *18 August 1772*

Whatever these deficiencies were, the move did not remedy them. Over the next fifteen years, the Bush and the Old Rose struggled until, following the bankruptcy of the then tenant, the lease was sold at a knock-down price to Hannah Chaplin, widow of John. She moved back to the Old Rose and closed the new one.

To complete the picture and add to the confusion, in 1844 the Old Rose, the one next to the Bush Inn, was closed down and the establishment moved across the road to Market Place, taking with it its old nomenclature the Olde Rose, which is the building that we know today.

The Olde Rose also has a singular claim to fame for having a (future) President of the United States of America as a customer. In 1997, one Barack Obama had arrived in England for his half-sister's wedding in Bracknell. Obama decided to join in the groom's stag night, which headed for Wokingham and ended at up the Rose. Obama evidently slid out the back door as a St Trinian's strippergram entered through the front door!

A Publican's Tale

If Molly Mogg deserves to be better known, so too does Paul Holton. His start in life was traumatic as he was a destitute who was taken in by the Coram Foundling Hospital in London. Such children were weaned and fostered by rural wet nurses, and as such on 29 January 1760 the month-old child was sent to live with Susana and William Houlton in Wokingham. It was their name that he would adopt as his own. Typically, when the orphaned child was around 6, they would be sent back to London to be apprenticed. But in Paul's case, a local man called John Grassingham applied for and was granted the right to take Paul on as an apprentice. According to the letter sent to the charity by John Bunce, the local voluntary overseer, John Grassingham had 'taken a liking to the child and have put him to scool [*sic*] at his expense and all most keeps him at his house. He is a wine merchant and distiller.'

Under the mentoring of John and latterly his wife Mary Grassingham, Paul set up a wine and brandy business from his house in 22 Market Place. By 1790, when Paul was 30, he had not only established himself as a successful businessman but also a well-respected man of the community. He was a Freeman of the Town, a burgess and then, in 1792, he was elected alderman. He became a churchwarden and a magistrate. All the while his business prospered. The wine vaults under his house in Market Place were a popular meeting place for the next couple of centuries. In turn, the vaults were owned by William Henry Ferguson, Robert Trickey Dunning and Daniel Norton Heron, and finally became Ferguson's Wine Vaults until they were closed in the 1970s.

Paul died in 1828 and in his will left a sum of money to the Foundling Hospital in London 'to which I bear the most grateful remembrance'. He is buried in All Saints Church with the following inscription:

Rose Street, seen here around 1880, has been home to at least seven public houses.

Near this place are interred the remains of Mr Paul Holton a capital Burgess of this Corporation for nearly 40 years. In the active scenes of life in which he was engaged the integrity of his character was highly respected and in his domestic circle he was beloved and esteemed for the cheerfulness and benevolence of his disposition.

If it were possible to step back in time to walk around Wokingham in the latter part of the eighteenth century it would be possible to visit half a dozen pubs that remain open today.

The Roebuck is probably one of our oldest pubs and pre-dates 1756, when we know it was owned by Martha Binfield, who inherited it from her mother. On the other side of the road is the Red Lion from about the same time, which until 1979 was adjacent to the King's Head. The licence plate for the last holder for the King's Head, W. Churchman, remains in place today above the shop door. The Ship Inn, on the edge of the old town, opposite the church, started out as a lodging house and became a functioning alehouse by about 1745.

Regulars at the Metropolitan public house, later Bar Fifty Six, in Rose Street, around 1920.

The Queen's Head on The Terrace is mentioned in the 1750s but in fact is housed in a fifteenth-century building, while the Duke's Head on the corner of Langborough Road is mentioned as a public house in 1795.

In terms of the other older pubs in town, it is only a few years since the demise of the Pin and Bowl in Finchampstead Road. The Pin was demolished in 1992 but we know that beer was being brewed there in 1722 and sold there in an alehouse in 1740.

Slightly out of town there is the Three Frogs, which also dates from this period although its internal and external appearance has been greatly altered over the last two centuries. On the Barkham Road there is Ye Olde Leathern Bottel, whose story starts in 1737, when it must have been a welcome sight for travellers through what was no doubt a wild and barren heathland. And then on Forest Row there is the Warren, which is advertised in the *Reading Mercury* of 15 November 1777, when a pigeon shoot was organised under the auspices of the publican, Mr Calloway.

Ayres and Hunter, in their seminal work, *The Inns and Public Houses of Wokingham*, refer to the period of 1830 to 1900 as the Railway Era. This was a time when many public houses and beer shops were opened as a result of the change in legislation as well as the opening up of the town itself by the arrival of the railway.

Needless to say, the Railway Hotel or Tavern or Tap opposite the station dates from this period. The pub had started life as a tavern but was then upgraded to a hotel and in 1856 was bought by the Wokingham Brewery. On the other side of the tracks, the now-closed Three Brewers opened its doors in 1858. The Two Poplars, originally the Engineer, was established to serve the 'navvies' working on the Reading to Guildford line extension.

As the nineteenth century matured into the twentieth, the number of new pub openings started to diminish and as we know in recent years numbers have declined as fashions and culture dictate. Nevertheless, the pubs of Wokingham remain both a pleasant place to spend a few hours with friends as well as linking us back to the near and more distant past.

Selected References

Ayres, D. and Hunter, J. (1994) *Inns and Public Houses of Wokingham*.

Bell, J. (2017*) A Short History of Wokingham*.

Sharnette, H. (2019) 'What contribution was made by the alehouse to the life of early modern towns?' Heather Sharnette. Available at: www.elizabethi.org. [Accessed 24 April 2019].

Young, B. (1995) 'Rags to Riches – Paul Holton – The Prologue'. *The Historian*, No. 8, 40–41.

Young, B. (1996) 'Rags to Riches – The Story of Paul Holton'. *The Historian*, No. 9, 2–11.

7

WOKINGHAM AT PLAY

The sporting instincts of the inhabitants of the district have always been well developed, although not necessarily applied in the right direction.

Arthur Heelas, 1928

The 'Wrong' Direction – Poaching and Hunting

The quiet respectability of today's town belies its more belligerent and, at times unsavoury, past. Environment, they say, plays a significant role in character formation, and this is probably the case for early Wokingham. The town's location on the edge of Windsor Forest seems, in the past, to have influenced the leisure or spare time activities of the local inhabitants.

One such activity could, of course, be poaching. Poaching for rabbits, hare, as well as an 'ill kill'd deer' as mentioned in Shakespeare's *The Merry Wives of Windsor*. The notoriety of the inhabitants of the forest had travelled to London's south bank. Perhaps one indication of the prevalence in this area of such 'sport' is The Overhangs, in Peach Street. These buildings date from the fifteenth century and are commonly believed to have housed the Windsor Forest Verderers' Court. This court would have dealt with misdemeanours such as poaching as well as the illegal felling of trees.

Having said that, the 'legitimate' hunting of deer, fox and other game by both the aristocratic or gentrified is also well represented in the town's past.

74

There were opportunities to hunt on the Billingbear Estate in the early part of
the twentieth century. T.B. Pither, who is standing on the left of the picture, was
the local butcher whose sign can still be read today on the side of a building in
Broad Street.

The Bramshill Hunt, which was subsequently renamed the Garth Hunt in
the 1850s, was active in and around Wokingham well into the twentieth
century. So much so that as late as 1921 a correspondent in the *Reading
Mercury* going by the name of 'Wryneck' would trace the track of the hunt
for avid followers:

> Going into Barkham Coombs the hounds found their first fox after 10
> minutes' drawing. There was such a cry, and they sent through cover at
> such a pace that there seemed every hope for a good scenting day. But it
> was not to be.

Bull-Baiting

One form of entertainment that is well documented is bull-baiting. There
is nothing unique about Wokingham having bull-baiting; it was a common
'sport' across the country, alongside bear-baiting and other similar activities.

The Garth Hunt continued through to the 1960s but this photograph from around 1900 shows one of the last meetings of the Royal Buckhounds in the Market Place.

However, the town's dubious claim to fame is that it was one of the last places in England for the activity to take place.

George Staverton was a butcher who chose to show his charitable credentials in a unique way. In his will dated 15 May 1661 he left the rental charge on his house in Staines to buy a bull annually for Wokingham. The beast was to be baited by dogs and then slaughtered, with the meat distributed amongst the town's poor. This was to be a gift of both food and entertainment.

Over time the trust accumulated other interests and by the eighteenth century it had increased to £20 per annum, which enabled two bulls to be purchased.

The bull-baiting took place on St Thomas's Day, 21 December, unless that fell on a Tuesday, market day, in which case it was held on the 20th.

The bull was bought to the Market Place a day earlier, paraded around the town and then locked up in an inn yard. In the morning the bull was fastened to an oak tree in the marketplace, which probably grew just in front of the Roebuck pub.

This nineteenth-century painting, which hangs in the town hall, shows the old guildhall to the right as a white building. The perspective, which seems to be taken from outside the Red Lion pub, makes the Market Place look bigger than it is today.

Supposedly, King George II visited Wokingham in the eighteenth century to see the baiting and stayed at the King's Head, a now-vanished pub that stood at No. 23 Market Place, which is next door to the Red Lion.

The event became highly organised with nominated dogs and special prizes, such as in 1774 when a prize of a Morocco collar was offered, stitched with silver and featuring a silver tag, a 'Guinea and half value'. Many of the dogs were trained on Langborough Common, where there was a large gipsy encampment on the south-east portion.

It is likely that most of the town and those living nearby would have been in attendance, including the more senior members of the corporation. The alderman himself, the appointed head of the town council, would sit with his friends in the large window of the old Red Lion Inn and give the signal for the sport to commence.

The event itself must have been riotous as in 1794 Elizabeth North was found dead, having been severely bruised as a result of getting too close to the baiting, and in 1808 Martha May was similarly killed as a result of being hurt in the fighting that took place in and around Market Place.

It is, therefore, no wonder that the more refined members of local society eventually began to see the event as having a detrimental effect on the town's image. As early as 1784 there were attempts to legislate against bull-baiting, but not everyone was so minded. William Taplin was a local surgeon and a purveyor of 'genuine horse medicines', and he wrote a letter to the *Reading Mercury* condemning bull-baiting in 1786. His reward for his concern for animal welfare was to be attacked and severely beaten by a group of local ruffians.

It was not until 1822 that bull-baiting was outlawed, but it would recur again as an impromptu event in 1835 and then as late as 1855.

Even after the baiting had come to an end, the charity first endowed nearly 400 years ago continued up to the start of the Second World War when meat and shoes were distributed to the poor children of the town.

And if bull-baiting was not your cup of tea, how about cockfighting round the back of the Red Lion, just along Cockpit Lane? For many years, cockfighting was extremely popular at all levels of society but eventually interest reduced, and the cockpits were turned into community gardens.

Boxing

If animal cruelty was not quite your thing then how about bare-knuckle fighting?

Tom Johnson was the bare-knuckle boxing champion of England in the latter part of the eighteenth century. He was a strong man who had worked as a London porter, but was somehow an intuitive and talented boxer. The combination was lethal and, over the course of his sporting career, he 'pulverised' one challenger after another. So much so that he ran out of likely competitors and had to look further afield, namely to Wokingham and a Bristol-based fighter called Bill Warr.

On 18 January 1787, Johnson took on Warr for the proclaimed Championship of England and a purse of £200 in the town square.

The fight lasted about ninety minutes and was pretty much one-sided. An account in the *Sporting World of Life in London and the Country* (26 April 1845) makes it sound like a scene from a *Carry On* movie:

In the first round, Warr found out that he had got a trump to deal with, by receiving a double from Johnson and immediately assumed the defensive. In fact, it was scarcely worth being called a fight … whenever Tom seemed likely to make a blow Bill War was on his knees praying … after an hour and half an ugly hit nailed him … he [Warr] insisted on calling 'foul'… and then instantly bolted, despite the remonstrances of his seconds to come back and finish the fight.

Healthy in Body and Mind

The development of more respectable leisure activities for the general population is related to two interrelated factors, namely economic and social. The growth of the middle class during the late Victorian period gave rise to a percentage of society who were free of the demands of agricultural and manual labour, had a level of disposable income and consequently had more free time to be occupied. Socially, there was a view that the middle and working class should not idly sit at home but be engaged in some activity for their betterment and for the good of the country and community. These trends led to the rapid expansion of reading rooms and apprentice halls as well as an increase in organised amateur sport from athletics through to cycling.

Not all activities were intellectual or strenuous; the town hall, for example, was a frequent venue for social functions of one kind or another, as indicated by a review of the events and 'appearances' that were staged there from 1870 and 1880.

Waxworks were popular with visits from Mullets, Sanger's as well as Hewlets, who had five vans loaded with displays. There were general entertainers such as Bosco the Conjuror, the Fat Lady Show, the Brooklyn Minstrels and Tyronees Singers. The local hunts held their balls, the Leigh Hunt in 1871 and the Garth Hunt in 1878. There was also a County Ball in 1870 and 1875. Then there were lectures from Reverend Charles Kingsley, the writer and rector of Eversley, and John Walter, owner of *The Times*. All good wholesome entertainment.

Sporting Endeavours

Around the town, there were also various sporting clubs and societies.

Wokingham Cricket Club was founded in 1825 but the first cricket match was, in fact, played a lot earlier, in 1767, with the first recorded match against Henley. At the start of the 1858 season, the members gathered to thank Mr Goodchild for the use of his land, Goodchild's Meadow or what was the Wellington Cricket Ground until the club moved out in 2012. At the end of the formal part of the meeting, 'several excellent songs were sung, and a most pleasant evening was spent, thus inaugurating the cricketing campaign in a manner that will long be remembered with satisfaction by all who were present'.

There was also a cycling club as early as 1858, when a race was held on 12 June:

A bicycle race, under the auspices of the Wokingham Cycling Club, took place on Wednesday evening, the course selected being from the 'Two Poplars' Inn to the letter-box at Finchampstead and back, a distance of almost five miles. There were 15 starters, the racing being against time and handicapped, two leaving the starting point together. The three following were declared the winners: F.J. Wells 1 (18m 10s., allowed 2m.); R. Simmons 2 (18m 12s., allowed 1m.); W. Scribbens 3 (17m 20s.). The quickest time made by the unsuccessful competitors was 16m 30s. and the longest 21m 35s. The first prize consisted of a silver-plated pint tankard; a pair of plated nut-crackers was the second, and the third was a pair of hair brushes and case. A smoking concert was afterwards held at the 'Bush' Hotel, the Mayor (Ald. Heron) in the chair.

Reading Mercury, *12 June 1858*

There were multiple football clubs, including Wokingham Town (founded in 1875), Wokingham Magpies, Wokingham Athletic Club, Wokingham Wednesday FC, Wokingham London Road Football Club and Wokingham Rovers Football Club. The latter was also known as the Unemployed Football Club in 1933. It was probably this profusion that led Arthur Heelas to comment that Wokingham had 'too many cricket, football and tennis clubs to produce a really strong team, but enough to prove the popularity of the sport'.

Both Wokingham Football Club and the cricket club have had their ups and downs over the years. The clubs were closed during hostilities in the First and Second World War and found it challenging to gain traction and members after that. The cricket club was in danger of being wound up in 1939, a consequence of low attendance after the war and the economic depression of the 1930s. Similarly, the football club struggled in the post-war era. The club acquired their own ground in Finchampstead Road with a pavilion that was opened in 1936; however, the costs of running the club and making necessary improvements became too much, and the ground was eventually sold in 1998. The club subsequently merged to become Wokingham & Emmbrook FC in 2004.

An annual tennis tournament started in 1881 and took place at the cricket ground in Wellington Road. Tennis clubs were popular in the town and included the Town and Milton Road Club as well as a Kestrels Lawn Tennis Club.

The Wokingham Club

A central fulcrum to sporting activities in the town was The Wokingham Club. This was an umbrella organisation for many sporting events in the town following the amalgamation of the cyclists' club and the Working Men's Club. The clubhouse, which offered billiard and snooker tables and hosted events such as whist drives and dances, was a gift from Howard Palmer. The house was located at Nos 19–21 Market Place and was latterly the base for the Wokingham Bowls Club, the green of which had initially been just out the back of the house. The club played a vital role in the life of the town both in peacetime and wartime, but eventually also succumbed to financial pressures and closed in 1960. The smart doorway entrance to the clubhouse is still visible today on the left of the building.

Back in the early 1930s, Alderman W.T. Martin (known as Billy Martin) had tried to persuade the council to build and open a swimming pool. Frustrated at the lack of vision or agreement, he did the next best thing and opened his own pool in 1934 in the garden of his house. There were two outdoor pools that epitomised the best design of the time with fountains, walkways and cascading rock pools. The council eventually came around and took over the responsibility of the pool until its closure in 1989.

Martin's Pool in the 1930s was the epitome of Art Deco design with its pools, fountains and lawns; it was the venue for swimming galas and beauty contests.

Cinema

Besides all the physical exertions, the town also boasted one of the first cinemas; the Wokingham Electric Theatre opened its doors on the afternoon of 10 March 1913. The exterior of the cinema is still clearly discernible at No. 10 Broad Street.

The early films were black and white and silent, and would have included *Dr Jekyll and Mr Hyde*, *David Copperfield* and, of course, those featuring Charlie Chaplin. Also known as the Savoy and then later as the Picture Palace, by 1937 the cinema faced competition with the opening of the Ritz Union Cinema in Easthampstead Road with its opening billing including *Girls' Dormitory*, a romance starring Simone Simon, and *Dimples* starring the better-known Shirley Temple.

The Ritz was once described as 'one of the finest cinemas in the South of England' and boasted air conditioning and lighting that dimmed. Tickets cost 6*d* (pence) in the stalls and 1*s* (shilling) in the balcony, leaving enough for a thrupenny ice cream in the interval.

In the days before pagers or mobile phones, reaching someone urgently was not always easy. However, if you were a senior manager at the Mid Wessex Water Company who held the key for turning on the excess water supply to fight a fire, then you could be pretty much assured that an impor-

Cubs, Scouts and Guides were very popular for Edwardian children; here the Boys' Brigade, 1st Wokingham Company, proudly pose for their inaugural group photograph.

tant message would get through. Such was the case for Mr E.J. Eving, who was enjoying an evening show at the Ritz on 5 May 1947 when a message was flashed on the screen saying he was urgently needed as there was a fire at Easthampstead Park Manor.

The Savoy eventually closed in 1951, while the Ritz prospered for many years offering the ubiquitous Saturday morning matinees for children, the Chums Club. It closed for a couple of years in the late 1970s for an attempted upgrade and then finally in 1986 became a bingo hall.

The Chums club was not the only leisure activity for children. In 1914 there was a Boys' Brigade as well as a Band of Lone Scouts. By 1921 a Girl Guides group had also been established alongside a Brownie and Cubs pack. It only took a few years for various such groups to materialise: in June 1929 children gathered at Glebelands, home of Sir Leslie and Lady Wilson, for a sports day under the heading of the RMSO. In attendance were Sea Scouts, the Mayor's Own 1st Wokingham Troop of Boy Scouts, the Rovers, the 1st Wokingham Cubs, 2nd Wokingham Cubs; Girl Guides, 1st Wokingham Brownies, 3rd Wokingham Brownies, 4th Wokingham Girl Guides (Bear Wood), 3rd Wokingham Wesleyan, and the 2nd Wokingham Girl Guides, Grosvenor School.

People gather to hear the local band as they celebrate Queen Victoria's Diamond Jubilee in 1897.

And finally, there was musical entertainment. At Christmas 1878, the Wokingham Amateur Band went around the town playing well-known Christmas hymns and carols, which according to the report in the *Reading Mercury* 'sounded very sweet in the still frosty night air'.

On another freezing day in January 1881, the Wokingham Brass Band accompanied people as they played and danced on the ice in Market Place. Moreover, of course, there were the church bands at St Paul's, All Saints and the Wesleyan Chapel Band of Hope as well as the local L Company Volunteer band. Playing music was so popular that, in 1892, there was a competition in Wokingham that eight bands entered.

The twentieth century saw the advent of television. The 1966 Football World Cup Final was watched by 32 million people in black and white and a similar number watched the funeral of Princess Diana in 1997. Besides these unique events, TV was a major pastime for the nation with 28 million watching the *Morecambe and Wise Christmas Show* in 1977. As the old millennium faded away, visits to the cinema were replaced by video cassette rental stores, but now they have gone as well. Participation in sporting and leisure activities may not have diminished, but they too have been subject to notable change. Nevertheless, on a Sunday morning watching today's Lycra-clad cyclists, it is interesting to speculate how many could cycle from the Two Poplars to Finchampstead and back in less than twenty minutes.

Selected References

Arborfield Local History Society, Memories – The Garth Hunt. Available at: www.arborfieldhistory.org.uk/memories_garth.htm [Accessed 8 June 2019].

Ayres, D. (1994) 'Bull Baiting'. *The Historian,* Nos 7, 13–18.

Baker, W. (1979) 'The Leisure Revolution in Victorian England: A Review of Recent Literature', *Journal of Sport History,* Vol. 6, No. 3, 76–87.

Bell, J. (2011) *A Short History of Five Wokingham Families.*

Dils, J. (1985) *An Account of Early Victorian Wokingham.*

Heelas, A. T. (1928) *Historical Notes on Wokingham.*

Theis, J. (2001) 'The 'ill kill'd' Deer: Poaching and Social Order in *The Merry Wives of Windsor'. Texas Studies in Literature and Language.* Vol. 43, No. 1, Renaissance Review: Wyatt, Spenser, Shakespeare, and Heywood, 46–73.

8

WOKINGHAM AT WORK

The Public are hereby requested to take notice that the FAIR will be held in the Market-place on the 10th of October, (old Michaelmas) to be continued yearly on that day for the sale of Cheese, all kinds of Merchandise, Cattle, etc. and also for the hiring of servants.

Reading Mercury, *22 September 1788*

A walk around the countryside and the remaining farms surrounding Wokingham today could suggest that its past was primarily agricultural in nature. Cheese and cattle are emphasised in the above notice from the end of the eighteenth century, seemingly bearing witness to an agrarian or pastoral economy. This assertion is only partially true. The area was heavily wooded ('hurst' is the Anglo-Saxon word for wood, hence Hurst and Sandhurst) and the soil was not sustainable for extensive arable farming. As such for much of its history, up until the modern era when advances in understanding enabled better yields, the focus was largely on less intensive working of the land.

In contrast to the area around Wokingham, the farmlands around Swallowfield, Arborfield, Shinfield and Binfield were primarily arable as their names suggest. Hereabouts, farming was small-scale and pastoral such as cattle, horses and sheep. Pigs seem to have played a significant role in the local economy and place names lend a hand in our orientation towards the past, for example, Bearwood (Boar-wood) and Hogwood.

Notwithstanding the above, Wokingham has a light industrial manufacturing heritage including a bell foundry, silk making and brickworks, as well
as tanning and brewing.

The 1788 notice for the fair partly points towards the present-day economy with its emphasis on retailing, 'the sale of ... all kinds of merchandise',
and services with its reference to 'the hiring of servants', which would have
included both domestic servants and farm labourers.

Farming

There were significant fluctuations in wheat prices in the seventeenth and
eighteenth centuries such that many agricultural labourers found themselves either out of work or on low and reduced wages. The Enclosure Acts
reduced the amount of land available for common grazing so few 'commons' remained in the vicinity of the town after the eighteenth century;
Langborough Common, for instance, remained open only until 1729. At the
same time, Wokingham was subject to the strict forest laws that controlled
rights to grazing, pannage, turf cutting and wood gathering. Mechanisation
followed, which improved productivity at the cost of a reduced need for
farm labour. As a result many parts of the county fell into general turmoil in
the 1830s with the Swing Riots, as disgruntled agricultural workers vented
their anger by, among other things, burning ricks; the farmers of Wokingham
formed their own Forest Association to combat these arson attacks. The
quaint image of the local peasant smoking his clay pipe and doffing his cap
dutifully to the benevolent landowner is to a greater or lesser extent a fiction
of the Edwardian period.

The area around Wokingham includes both a fertile loam soil as well as sand
and gravel. This patchiness has meant that arable farming, of wheat, oats and
barley, was typically not particularly productive and for the main part of its
history around 60–70 per cent of agriculture was livestock and the majority
cattle. In 1607, Richard Palmer's cattle herd was assessed at £94 per annum,
while the farming interests of Thomas Syms were valued at £89 and included
eleven cows, one bull, twelve bullocks, five calves, seven horses, and 121 sheep
and ewes (the average was thirty, so this was a big flock) and ten pigs.

In the Elizabethan period, more than 40 per cent of local inhabitants were
engaged in farming; this compared with 20 per cent involved in clothing and

Cattle market day, around 1880, no doubt providing a flow of customers to the Red Lion pub on the right-hand side.

cloth making, including silk, and 16 per cent in tanning; the remainder were employed in various other tasks from retailing to bell foundry work.

The town was endowed with a weekly market and two annual fairs, but these did not seem to have been well utilised. According to the *General View of the Agriculture in Berkshire* by William Fordyce Mavor for the early part of the nineteenth century:

> The fairs belonging to this town are most unaccountably neglected, or at least as they ought to be. Standing in a neighbourhood where many sheep and other cattle are bred, possessing a fine spacious Market Place and surrounded by enclosures, where sellers might comfortably and cheaply be accommodated during the continuance of affairs; it is really surprising that Oakingham has not become a mart for Forest stock, as well as for cattle of every kind from other parts of the kingdom.

A comparative study between 1851 and 1901 shows the numbers engaged in agriculture falling dramatically as the town's population doubled.

	1851	1901
Farmers	41	23
Farm Bailiffs	9	5
Agricultural Workers	419	223
Total Population	3,752	6,012

Having said that, as late as 1903 it was possible to identify seventeen farms in and around the town; there was a nursery and poultry farm in London Road as well as cattle at Wiltshire Road, Emmbrook, Matthewsgreen and Norris Barn farms. Farming remained close to the heart of the town, but its importance was rapidly diminishing.

The agricultural situation after the First World War did not improve. As people started to get their lives back to normal, there was heavy flooding across the county, and an outbreak of foot and mouth disease severely impacted dairy farming.

By the middle of the twentieth century, many of the farms were being converted to housing estates, such as at Dowles Green, Woosehill and Rances Farm. The pressure on land for new houses continues into the twenty-first century.

Silk Weaving

A far more curious and unexpected occupation was silk weaving. Silk and silk manufacture had travelled eastwards during the medieval period. It was, of course, greatly prized. The Byzantine empire had for centuries been the source of much of the silk that made its way to English shores. Greece and then Sicily became manufacturing centres, and the industry spread out through Italy and France in the fourteenth century. By the sixteenth century, France and Flanders had an established and thriving industry, but religious persecution of the Protestant Huguenots led to an exodus to England of refugee weavers from 1585 onwards.

The first reference to silk production in Wokingham is in 1616 when Jane Barber engaged an apprentice to knit silk stockings. She took out a bond on the Wokingham Corporation to formalise and legitimise the apprenticeship. In the same year, John Ticknor who had lived in Rose Street on the corner of Cross Street, died and in his will called himself a 'silk knitter'.

These two events heralded the start of the industry. Silk farming in the town developed sufficiently over the next couple of decades such that in 1625 the Wokingham Corporation issued a series of bylaws to the effect that 'poor people', most likely those in the workhouse, were set to work knitting silk stockings and, if they refused, the alderman could commit them to the 'house of correction'. This association between the workhouse and silk weaving is reinforced in 1629 when Richard Thomas took as an apprentice 'a poor child to serve him at the trade of silk knitting'. Nearly fifty years after Jane Barber took on her apprentice, in 1662 Henry Dearing would list on his marriage certificate his occupation as 'silk weaver'. The industry had a tenuous root in the town.

The production of silk is not, however, straightforward. Silk comes from silkworms. Silkworms are not native to England, nor is the mulberry bush that they need for sustenance. The first attempts at manufacturing the raw material must have been very frustrating. To begin with, James I distributed more than 100,000 black mulberry bushes to encourage the development of the trade; high-quality silk comes from worms fed on the white mulberry bush; those fed on black mulberry bush leaves produce inferior quality silk. The mulberry bush needs a warm climate; England suffered the worst of the Little Ice Age from around 1680 and 1730. Much of the silk was therefore imported in a raw state in bales from Turkey.

This raw material needed to be spun and in 1771 Clement Cruttwell, a local surgeon, his brother William and their brother-in-law, Thomas Brooks, set up a factory or spinning mill in the town, just behind the shop fronts on Peach Street. The business struggled for several reasons: the essential raw materials would not have been cheap, and they had to make continued payments to the poor house in exchange for the incumbents knitting the silk.

The Grout brothers established an additional factory in the town in the early part of the nineteenth century. The industry, by this time, was under assault from cheap imports and the factory was closed in 1832, subsequently destroyed by fire in 1855 and then replaced by a sawmill. In 1833, a Parliamentary report identified that the 'town has no manufacturing'. Indeed, neither Pigot's nor Kelly's Directories for the mid-century reveal anything other than a Victorian service economy of bakers, blacksmiths and butchers.

Despite its seeming longevity over two centuries, the heyday of the silk industry was short-lived. Indeed, looking at it with the benefit of hindsight it never was more than a few attempts to exploit a specific business opportunity; it is probable that there were more people engaged in the less esoteric and more mundane wool knitting from the far more prevalent, and less fussy, sheep.

Nevertheless, it is cheering to know that the last of the older black mulberry bushes survived in the gardens of The Elms until as recently as 2015.

Brewing

Over the years the citizens of Wokingham have enjoyed the pleasures of a multitude of inns and pubs and, remarkably, some of the oldest are still with us. Accompanying and supplying these outlets were the breweries. While Wokingham has never generated a major national or even regional brewery, for some time large firms owned by locally based families held sway over much of the town's alcohol – especially beer – consumption.

In all likelihood, beer was probably brewed in and around the town during the medieval period, but it isn't until the seventeenth century that it is possible to put a name to any individual brewers. Robert and John Hawes are the first brewers that can be identified, but the larger breweries start to emerge in the 1760s with the Webb family.

Father and son, both called James, between them owned twelve tied public houses. Among them were The Leathern Bottle, The Roebuck, The Red Lion, and The Duke's Head. The family lived at Beaches Manor, and the brewhouse sits on the Reading Road, today serving as the Masonic Hall. Mavor, in his *General View*, offers some praise for the beer, no doubt based on personal consumption: 'The Brewery of James Webb, Esq. is pretty extensive; and produces a wholesome and pleasant beverage, not inferior to any in the county.'

Although the male Webb line petered out, a daughter married into another brewing family, the Haywards, and it was to this family that James Webb, the younger, sold the business in 1821.

The Haywoods grew the business until, by the 1850s, it was the dominant brewery in the town with more than a third of all outlets under their control; a sizeable percentage of outlets in the town were simple beer shops. However, the business overreached itself and in 1856 it collapsed.

The enterprise seems to have been too large for any nearby brewery to purchase in totality and so it was sold off effectively in 'parcels'. A local plumber called Robert Trickey Dunning bought one of these lots, namely the Chair at No. 23 Denmark Street. Dunning had previously managed the Red Lion in Market Place as well as Ferguson's Wine Vaults, so he was no stranger to the victuallers' trade. His plans for the Chair were grand. The pub was renamed the Wellington Arms in honour of the Iron Duke, Dunning then went further and built the Wellington Brewery on land he had bought behind the pub. The business prospered, so much so that in 1877 Robert's son, Thomas, decided to retire and sell up; anecdotally Thomas had become disillusioned about the morality of selling alcohol. By that time, alongside the Wellington Arms and the brewery, the family owned seven other establishments in and around the town with an annual production of more than 300,000 pints.

The Headington family bought the Wellington Brewery business for £11,400. The brewery stayed in the Headington family for the next couple of generations and they successfully expanded it to fifteen freehold properties, including the Greyhound at Finchampstead. It was acquired in 1921 by Ashby's of Staines. Their interest was in the outlets, the pubs, and as such they let the brewery falter and close down a few years later.

The town had another, smaller, brewery, the Wokingham Brewery, which had closed a few years earlier around 1915 following about 100 years in business. The much larger Brakspear Brewery of Henley-on-Thames acquired the Wokingham Brewery. As such, the start of the twentieth century saw the large brewery operations leave the town, and with it the end of an era.

Bell Making

Wokingham was also home to a far less secular industry, namely bell making. The impetus for what is a complicated and specialised activity is not known, but the earliest attributed bell from the Wokingham foundry can be dated to very early in the town's history, in the early fourteenth century. The name of the first founder in Wokingham is not known, and these first manufacturing attempts produced inferior bells. Having said that, the founding enterprise, whether run by the original manufacturer or someone else, did not falter and as the century progressed the quality of the bells produced started to improve.

Roger Wolgrave and William Landen are the earliest known individuals who established a foundry in the town in about 1422. By 1424 Landen was in sole charge and continued to run the business through to 1442, when his son, Roger, took over and managed it through to 1482. As the quality improved, so too did the firm's reputation and the business thrived as more prestigious clients took their requirements to the Wokingham foundry. In 1475 Roger hired William ate Lee to take a bell to replace an older one at Eton College near Windsor Castle. Roger Landen was now confident enough and sufficiently proud of his craftsmanship to stamp his initials, RWL, on each one. Roger Landen had two sons, but, around 1484, just before his death, the foundry was sold to a John Michel, who lived in Wokingham. Michel would use the Lion head mark on the bells as his maker's sign.

Under the management of the Michel family, the importance of the Wokingham foundry diminished. In 1495, two men rode from Thame to Wokingham to ensure that a fractured bell was readily and adequately repaired. The men were forced to return with their quest unfulfilled as the foundry could not be found because most of the activity had moved to Reading.

The local business never returned to the height of its success and was probably on a far smaller scale than previously. Nevertheless, a foundry remained in the town into the seventeenth century, run for a time by Fulk Mitchel (John Michel's son). However, the operation was up against stiff competition and went through changes of hands until around 1624 when the then owner, Richard Eldridge, died, and the foundry was closed.

Names can be deceiving as Bell Foundry Lane is not the location of the bell foundry; it is the location of the farm owned by William Landen. The precise location of the foundry is not known but can be deduced from various maps and documents such that it is reasonably safe to say that it was towards the rear of Nos 11–13 Broad Street. The site could have backed onto Rose Street, which would have been enclosed at that time, so everything would probably have come through a main entrance on Broad Street. It is hard to imagine the heat, the smoke and the noise that would accompany such an operation; the hustle and bustle as raw materials were delivered, and the waste removed. Then the finished product would be sent out to customers around the county – a hive of activity in the very heart of the town.

Tanning

Sheep farming in the locality supported the woollen industry in the town. There were also oats and barley grown nearby for the brewers, and, of course, there were cattle. The dairy cattle would have provided milk and cheese, and some would have been farmed for their meat, although red meat was a luxury for the majority of people. Eventually, the animal would become the raw material for the tanning trades.

There is no way to describe the tanning process that makes it sound glamorous. It was a dirty and very smelly business. The animal hides would be delivered and the raw flesh scraped off. The hides were then soaked in a solution that was extremely potent made up of urine, dogs' excrement and chicken droppings. Subsequently, the hides were placed in pits for up to six months of 'pickling'. The stench would have been incredible.

Wokingham had at least two tanneries, one each end of the town, so that no matter which way the wind was blowing it would be carrying the 'subtle perfumes' of the works of Messieurs Marlowe and Twycross.

Both of these tanneries were located along the Emm Brook. Richard Marlowe most likely was conducting his business as early as 1595. A descendant of his called John was assessed for taxation in 1635 for a tannery. The business and accompanying buildings were sold in 1690 by William Marlowe to John Symons, a glove maker of Wokingham. The sale included a plot of land employed as a tan yard and included 'the tan-pits and cisterns there planted and being also the bark mill and all utensils belonging to the tannery'. The site was where the Emm Brook crosses the Finchampstead Road.

There is an anecdotally informed view or at least supposition that the long association of the brook and the Marlowe family caused it to be named Marlowe's Brook. A cartographer, in the early seventeenth century or in the eighteenth century, either lazy or cramped for space, shortened this on a map to M. Brook, which is possibly where the Emm Brook name originates. If not true, it remains a good story nevertheless!

Sometime in the early eighteenth century, the Symons or Simmonds family opted out of the tannery business. In 1722 John Simmonds junior mortgaged the site for £200. At that point in time, the landholding was described as having been an orchard or garden and was the location of a

This is the Tan House on Barkham Road, alongside a free-flowing Emm Brook.

brewhouse and a mill house. Within a year John Simmonds was bankrupt, and the site was sold again. The cottage became a public house, the Pin and Bowl, which continued serving customers up until 1992, when it was closed.

On the other side of town, Richard Miller owned a tannery on the Emm Brook in 1610, close to Tan House Lane. The tanner lived at Highbridge House, which was adjacent to a high bridge crossing marshy Emm Brook. At some point in the eighteenth century, James Twycross bought the tannery. James came from a family of fellmongers and tanners who dealt in the processing of sheep and cattle hides. The family business prospered such that by the 1850s James Twycross & Sons was employing forty-three workers. The tannery was auctioned at the Rose Hotel in Wokingham in September 1922 and was sold for £2,300; it was demolished sometime in 1960. The pollution seeping into the Emm Brook must have been excessive. Those that hark back to the simplicity of olden days might care to contemplate the smell and noise and general pollution that former industries would have generated.

Brickworks

Wokingham enjoyed a manufacturing boom of a kind in the latter part of the Victorian era when there were several manufacturers of bricks along the Emm Brook.

Thomas Lawrence's brickyards had the lengthiest history. Lawrence's works were just west of Molly Millars Lane alongside Eastheath Avenue. Lawrence was a successful businessman who had sites in Swinley, Warfield, Pinewood and Easthampstead as well as Wokingham. He was also a draper with a large department store in Bracknell High Street. The Wokingham site sprawled over an impressive 58 acres and included a 60ft-deep pit, two Hoffman kilns, ten workers' cottages, and chimneys reaching 200ft into the Wokingham skyline. The yard was producing 10 million bricks a year; some were handmade bearing the mark 'T.L.B.' and others machine cut marked '★WK★'. The site also had its own tramway, crossing Molly Millars Lane and the Emm Brook before joining up with the main line just outside the station. Bricks were being produced through to the 1960s, when a flood caused extensive damage and the site was finally closed down.

Lawrence's was not the only brickyard. Bricks had been produced at Carey Road as early as 1870 but this only lasted until 1886. Thomas Marley Westcott was making bricks closer to the station at Oxford Road from around the end of the nineteenth century up until 1910, when the business faltered. Out of town, there was a kiln at Kiln Ride, off Nine Mile Ride, and another on the Reading Road opposite the Rifle Volunteer pub. Edmund W. Collis and Company was making bricks at Toutley Road as late as the 1940s.

The noise and dust from the yards must have been significant and added to the general busyness of the town. The chimneys would have been blowing out coal-produced smoke for the better part of the day, winter and summer. The tramway to and from the station would have added to the clatter and grating as the bricks were shipped away.

Over the years, Wokingham has not been isolated from the general impacts of the economy. In 1809 Thomas Mann of Reading wrote that: 'Wokingham itself … is the most depressing place you ever saw, where poverty seems to have taken up her abode and from whence the energies of the British character seem to have fled.'

The situation did not get any better later in the nineteenth century as the country, and the town, entered an economic depression after the Boer Wars.

The view along Broad Street in the 1920s seems to be subdued and the men appear to be idling around the wooden case or resting between exertions.

Like many places in the 1930s, the town had a high number of people out of work. In 1930 the council supported the establishment of the Unemployed Association of Wokingham. In 1932, fifty families were invited to Christmas dinner courtesy of the local Salvation Army.

The general affluence around the town today easily obscures some of the hardships and poverty that earlier inhabitants had to endure.

In the twenty-first century, agriculture remains present around the town but less critical to the local economy and employing fewer inhabitants of the town and district. There remains no manufacturing in the town today. No tanning, bell making or brewing. Lush coachworks, suppliers to royalty, closed. The timber yard and the sawmill that were originally located at the back of Peach Street are no more. The brickfields near the station are gone. And the wire rope factory ceased production many years ago. The economy of Wokingham is effectively wholly service and retail-based, with many residents commuting to Reading or London or homeworking for multinational technology-based companies.

Selected References

Allington, P., Dawe, P., Hoare, B., Holland, C., King, P. (ed.), Lowe, K., Lowe, L., McLaren, J., Mitchell, C., and Watts, J. (2016) *Late Victorian Wokingham*, The Wokingham Society.

Ayres, D. (1990) 'The Wokingham Bell Foundry'. *The Wokingham Historian*, No. 1, 7–14.

Bell, J. (2015) *A Short History of Five Wokingham Families.*

Hosking, R. (1990) 'The Wellington Brewery'. *The Wokingham Historian*, No. 9, 12–26.

9

WOKINGHAM AT WAR

We've watched you playing cricket; And every kind of game.
At football, golf, and polo; You men have made your name.
But now your country calls you; To play your part in war,
And no matter what befalls you; We shall love you all the more.
So come and join the forces; As your fathers did before.

'Your King and Country Want You', a British popular song from 1914

The War Front

The English Civil War lasted from 1641 to 1651, between the Parliamentarians and Royalists, that is the Roundheads and the Cavaliers. Civil war divides the population into two camps, it divides families, and it divides a country. Wokingham, for several years of the English Civil War through to 1643, was located in a contested area on one of the primary geographic dividing lines.

Many issues prompted the Civil War and several of them resonated seriously with the people of Wokingham. Ship Money was an unpopular form of taxation that was levied on the more affluent population. In Wokingham, this amounted to around £100 per year, which would equate to £25,000 in today's world. War with Scotland led to troops being billeted in town to the cost of £77. And then Wokingham was within Windsor Forest and to squeeze every last penny the forest laws were rigorously enforced, and more common land was enclosed.

Nevertheless, when the Civil War broke out, Sir Richard Harrison, High Steward of Wokingham, with Richard Beaver, raised three troops of horse in support of the king. One contributing factor might have been that the commander-in-chief of the Berkshire Royalist troops was a local man. Major-General Sir Richard 'Moses' Browne was the son of John Browne of Wokingham. Browne would eventually take the lead position in Charles II's triumphant procession into London at the Restoration.

In Reading, on the other hand, Henry Marten raised forces for Parliament. The Royalist forces moved on Windsor and then London, only to be rebuffed, forced to retreat and establish themselves in Reading. The Royalists destroyed bridges across the Loddon and Thames to slow down the Parliamentarian advance, which made travel and trade across the area difficult and hazardous.

The Parliamentarians recaptured Reading later in 1643, only to withdraw to the east of the town as an epidemic hit, leaving Wokingham once again cast adrift between the two forces.

Life became harder for the townsfolk by the ongoing requests, effectively raids, to take horses and food and whatever else was needed, while marauding troops harassed the countryside:

> Friday 20th October … John Lane came from Okeingham and saith that hee sawe about 30 of the cavallyers there this afternoon, and whoe came in to warne the townsmen to make ready their hay, firewood and bedding for there were 80 carts coming to fetch it away, and that hee heares that they threaten to burn the towne that night.
> *The Diary of Sir Samuel Luke, Scoutmaster General for the Parliamentary Forces*

The report was correct. On 22 October, four houses were burnt down in Wokingham, and within a week '30 howses and outhowses burnt in Okeingham and almost all in Twyford'. Thirty houses represented around a half of the town. This devastation was the nadir for Wokingham as the fighting moved west and the Parliamentarians strengthened their hold on the area.

However, the local economy was severely weakened and the harvests for the next few years were substantially reduced as a consequence of the so-called

Little Ice Age, which was characterised by freezing winters and wet summers. All of this meant that for the local people there was a great risk of famine.

The times must have been extremely hard for the inhabitants of Wokingham. The town had experienced a direct taste of war, and it would take two generations before it was back on its feet. As late as 1704, it would appear that Wokingham was still struggling to come out from the shadow of the Civil War as the townspeople were finding it difficult to raise the necessary funds to pay for the repair of the damaged town hall.

The Home Front

Wokingham in 1914 was a pleasant place to live. The only crime reported in the local newspaper concerned a drunk and disorderly soldier and the arrest of Frederick George Langman for stealing eight posts. Most of the news involved the lighter side of life in a small market town, in the Home Counties during the Edwardian era.

In May, the Marchioness of Downshire had opened a bazaar to raise money for the local fire brigade. A day trip to Boulogne was advertised in the *Reading Mercury* on 1 August. There was the Oddfellow's Fete, a Friendly Society, held on 8 August with displays of fruits and vegetables. There were numerous reports on sporting activities, including the summer victory of Wokingham Wednesdays Cricket team against Easthampstead on 22 August by twelve runs.

In the midst of this normality was the build-up and declaration of war on 4 August. On 20 August, at a meeting in the town hall, Colonel Colebrooke Carter explained that Lord Kitchener had asked for more men and that it was 'the duty of every man and woman to do all that was possible to enable him to have a force at his disposal'.

Wokingham responded in kind and a recruitment office was opened with immediate effect. A civil guard was established that would drill at Langborough Recreation Ground starting on the first Wednesday in September.

And then as the month progressed news of the first casualties came through:

Lt. Frederick de Vere Allfrey, 9th Lancers, the only son of Frederick Vere Allfrey and grandson of Mrs Bruce of Arborfield Court, was killed aged 22. A German shot him after he had dismounted to extract a lance from a wounded comrade's leg.

This was to be the last anachronistic 'lance-on-lance' battle of the First World War, in September 1914 at Moncel.

September also saw the arrival of the first refugees. The German invasion of Belgium had prompted Britain's entrance into the war. Over the next three years, nearly 250,000 Belgian refugees would come to England and a few would find their way to Wokingham.

The first group to arrive were a group of ten little girls, the youngest no more than 3. The girls walked along Peach Street from the station and down to the French Convent at No. 73 Easthampstead Road. Shute End House was made available for the arrival of more refugees with a Mademoiselle Luitzen in charge. Red Lodge, on the London Road, was also opened up, as was Frogmore, No. 48 Sturges Road, as the 'Convent School for the Belgians'. The arrival of outsiders into the town was to become an emergent theme for the duration.

On 24 January 1915, more than 1,000 men were billeted in the town from the 10th Northumberland Fusiliers. A further 1,100 arrived the same weekend from the 13th Durham Light Infantry. In March more than 2,000 men from the 6th Buffs (East Kent Regiment) were quartered in the town. And then again at the end of the month 2,000 men from the 5th Berks and 7th Norfolks.

The town would provide entertainments of various kinds for these soldiers in transit, and inevitably friendships were struck up; perhaps no more poignantly than between a young Wokingham girl and a soldier of the Norfolks, for, according to a report in the *Reading Mercury* on 21 August:

Miss A. Paice of Goodchild Road, Wokingham has just had her photograph which was found on the battlefield, returned to her. The Censor enclosed it in a letter from Private Palmer to his wife at London Road, Wokingham, and a note was appended by the Censor asking Mrs Palmer to forward the photograph to its owner, whose address was written on the back. The photograph was given to a private in the 7th Norfolks when he was billeted in Wokingham and who is reported missing.

While many of these soldiers were passing through on the way to the front, others who had been wounded were shipped back home and stayed to recuperate for weeks or months. Bear Wood became a convalescent hospital for Canadians; in 1917, there were 900 Canadian patients staying at the park.

Church House in Easthampstead Road had been converted to a hospital for non-contagious diseases at the start of the war, but by the summer of 1916 it was regularly receiving wounded from the front.

Philanthropic support for the 'boys' took multiple unique paths. Mrs Dunne, the wife of Major Dunne of Toutley Hall, started a collection of fresh eggs to be sent to the wounded at home and overseas. Between 1915 and 1918 when the war came an end, 70,652 eggs were collected and sent from Toutley Depot!

The day 7 June 1916 was declared 'Fag Day', with the specific objective of collecting cigarettes and tobacco to be sent to the front line. In total nearly 3 million cigarettes, 180,000 cigars and 2,000 pipes were donated in twelve months within Berkshire.

During the First World War, despite the presence of trucks, aircraft and tanks, the main beasts of burden were horses, donkeys and mules. Incredibly, some 1 million horses were actively engaged in the war effort, and many passed through Wokingham along Barkham Road on their way to the Army Remount Depot for horses at Arborfield.

The Remount Depot had been opened in 1904 with the acquisition of land in and around Biggs Farm, from whence Biggs Lane gets its name. As the war progressed, the acreage at Arborfield was increased, and farmland was acquired that extended from Langley Common Road to Commonfield Lane. At that time stabling was expanded to accommodate a further 600 horses. Many of these horses would arrive back from France to Wokingham station and be driven along Barkham Ride late at night or early morning. Despite the amount of new building, the infirmary stables used by the equine vets for their patients remain as a protected building and, at the time of writing, there are plans for statues of a horse to be positioned outside a newly built development.

Meanwhile, the concerts and the dances and the whist drives continued. And so too did the number of casualties and wounded. Nearly 200 young men from Wokingham were killed, that is 200 out of a population of around 5,000.

Here is the story of just one taken from the excellent *Wokingham Remembers* archives:

The crowds were out in force in Market Place for the peace celebrations to mark the end of the First World War in 1919.

Frederick Fullbrook. Died 13th August 1915
Frederick was one of the eight children of Elizabeth and Walter Fullbrook of Havelock Place, Wokingham. He was only 16 when he died, sailing to Gallipoli on board the 'Royal Edward' troopship as part of the re-enforcements to the troops there. He was a member of the 2nd Battalion Hampshire Regiment, and he was lost together with about 1000 other troops. On the 13th August 1915, the troop transport 'Royal Edward' was steaming towards Mudros, carrying men and supplies for the Gallipoli campaign, when she was torpedoed by a German Submarine, the U-14, and became the first troopship to be sunk in the First World War.

The First World War had erased Edwardian vanities. To add to the misery, the Spanish flu followed the men home from the trenches. And a decade later, as things might have been expected to be getting back to normal, the depression hit, and many were out of work.

Nevertheless, the resilience of Wokingham inhabitants was such that by 1939 the local newspapers were once more filled with sporting results. Wallingford beat Wokingham by six wickets on 26 August, but the tennis team won by five matches against Windlesham. On other pages, Perkins Brothers of Wokingham were offering for sale a 1938 Series Austin Big 7 four-door saloon, finished blue, very little used, for £110, and the Ritz cinema was showing *I Am the Law* with Edward G. Robinson.

The anticipation of war in 1939 was high. Air Raid Precaution wardens were already established in Wokingham as early as 1938, with Wokingham designated as No. 3 District and divided into six posts with volunteer wards already in position. The Women's Land Army was announced, and there was a trickle of young women onto the farms around the town; by 1941 there would be 51,000 Land Girls taking up the challenge. Blackout precautions were in place from 1 September.

Whereas in 1914 the announcement of war was proclaimed at the town hall, by 1939 it was the radio and the famous broadcast of Prime Minister Chamberlain that gave notice of what was to come:

> This morning the British Ambassador in Berlin handed the German Government a final note stating that, unless we heard from them by 11 o'clock that they were prepared at once to withdraw their troops from Poland, a state of war would exist between us. I have to tell you now that no such undertaking has been received, and that consequently, this country is at war with Germany.

The first evacuees arrived in Wokingham from London as part of Operation Piper on 8 September. The government had announced the evacuation on 31 August; there was a fear that aerial bombardment of cities and towns as witnessed during the recent Spanish Civil War would commence as soon as the war was declared. The next day, 9 September, the quietness of the town was shattered by an air-raid siren that blasted across the local vicinity.

There would be an ebb and flow of evacuees into the town over the next four years. Some would stay a few weeks before returning home, others would remain for many years. Some were ill-fed and dirty; others were polite and bright. The children attended the local schools for lessons; the local children in the morning and the evacuees in the afternoon.

Arborfield Remount had disbanded in 1937 and became the home of the Army Technical School, morphing into the REME Training College in 1946. During the war it served as a staging post for soldiers on their way overseas. Meanwhile, down the road in Finchampstead, the Special Operations Executive was training its agents in map reading and endurance at West Court House.

Seven air-raid shelters were created to cope with the surprising 236 bombs that fell in the district. Reading sustained damage but there was only one instance of a deadly raid. This was on Wednesday, 10 February 1943 when a lone Dornier bomber dropped four bombs.

Wokingham had a couple of near misses. The first occasion was when a bomb fell on what was to become St Crispin's school playing field. The second occurrence was on 4 October 1940, when a 1,000lb high-explosive bomb and four oil bombs fell on Wokingham. Walter Percy Fenwick spotted the Junkers Ju 88 German bomber that dropped the bombs. Walter was a postman better known as 'Old Havelocker'. He had been out on his rounds delivering post to the residence of Miss E. Tice, niece of Lord Downshire of South Lodge, Easthampstead. As the plane swooped low down over the treetops, 'Old Havelocker' clambered into the back of his van with Miss Tice and slammed the doors shut, just in time to avoid being killed by the explosion and shrapnel. The Junkers was shot down as it flew back over the Hog's Back at Guildford.

The billeting of troops in the town, which was a hallmark of the First War World, did not generally take place, but there was a steady influx of soldiers passing through Wokingham. This came to a peak during the first week of June 1944. American, Canadian and Dutch soldiers were accommodated throughout the town; the roads were busy with trucks carrying soldiers and equipment along Denmark Street to Eversley and beyond; the build-up for the D-Day landings in Normandy had begun.

The end of the war was initially marked soberly by a service in Market Place followed by the crowd listening to the broadcast of the king's speech. But as the evening wore on things livened up:

The large crowds in the (Market) Square joined in the dancing which had spontaneously commenced to the sounds of relayed dance music, the scene being illuminated by flood lighting from the Rose Hotel. The fact that the 'dance floor' consisted of recently laid gravel appeared to be no deter to the dance whose numbers increased as the public houses closed. Fireworks and thunder flashes made an effective contribution to the unusual (for Wokingham) spectacle, and at midnight everyone joined in singing God Save the King.

The Wokingham Times and Weekly News, *11 May 1945*

Selected References

Arborfield Local History Society, The Remount Depot. Available at: www. arborfieldhistory.org.uk/WW1/WW1_Remount_Depot.htm [Accessed 8 June 2019].

Ayres, D. (1990) 'The Burninge of Okeingham'. *The Wokingham Historian,* No. 2, 8–14.

Bell, J. (2009) *Wokingham Remembers the Second World War.*

Bell, J. (2014) *A Chronology of Wokingham Home Front During W.W.1.*

Goatley, K. (2004) 'Wokingham: the town of my life'. *The Wokingham Society.*

Goatley, K. (2006) 'Bygone days in Wokingham'. *The Wokingham Society.*

Lea, J., Goldschmied, R. and Parker, B. (ed.) (1995) 'Wokingham from Elizabeth I to Cromwell'. *The Wokingham Society.*

Wokingham Remembers. Available at www.wokinghamremembers.com [Accessed 25 January 2019].

10

WOKINGHAM AT PRAYER

Sacred to the memory of Edward Horne who died in this his native town on the 18th day of December 1857 in the 90th year of his age, esteemed and well respected by all who knew him. 'To do justly, to love mercy and to walk humbly with his God' were through life the animating principles of him whose death is above recorded. 'Go ye and do likewise'.

Plaque on north wall of the Lady Chapel in All Saints Church

Faith and Hope

Anyone coming into town by car, from the east, along London Road, will pass the squat All Saints Church as they turn into Peach Street. Arriving at Wokingham station, train passengers surely note the elegant spire of St Paul's that lifts itself up and over the car park and reaches skyward.

In the town centre, there is the Methodist Church, the Baptist Church and Corpus Christi Catholic Church as well as the Salvation Army in Sturges Road.

It is possible to consider these as the primary religious establishments of Wokingham, which are interwoven with the history of the town.

All Saints is intimately bound up with the establishment of Wokingham. The original Anglo-Saxon chapel would probably have been a hut in a 'clearing in the woods' to which the local people would come for prayer and succour. The town would have grown up around the chapel, probably along Rose Street, and then expanded once the right to hold a market had been granted in 1219. The names of some of the earliest ministers to the chapel are known; these were Alerud, his son Robert and then Robert's brother Godefridus in 1160.

After the Norman Conquest, the chapel was dedicated as a church in about 1190 to All Saints by Bishop Hubert of Old Sarum. The 'tenants' of the new church were Hamo, who was appointed in 1220, and the chaplain was Phillip, who paid Hamo 10 marks a year for the privilege. Johannes de Wokingham followed Hamo in about 1300.

At the time of Johannes, the church seems to have been impoverished with only one old and slightly tatty surplice, the white tunic worn by clergy. However, things went from bad to worse when Stephen Cartwright was parish chaplain in around 1410. He seems to have had an affair with a parishioner, Alice Stephens, he openly discussed people's confessions and used the reredos (the ornamental screen covering the wall at the back of an altar) to make a table. His shepherding of the local parishioners also left much to be desired; trees were cut down in the churchyard, marriages were conducted without banns, and Richard Cubbel admitted being a devil worshipper.

The backdrop to this period is the Black Death, which was a bubonic plague pandemic that reached England in June 1348. The specific impact on Wokingham is not known, but across the county maybe as many as 50 per cent of the population died. There is no reason to assume that Wokingham escaped this devastation. As the country and town started to recover towards the end of the century, this was also the period when the church was extensively rebuilt, and the first charitable endowments in the town were made.

The improprieties of the church did not improve a great deal. William Robson was curate in 1538 and Hugo Wyrall in 1546. Around this time, the church did not have its own Bible, the 'new' church was damp and cold inside, and outside in a general state of disrepair, while a parishioner, Alicia Larkington, was found wandering the graveyard drunkenly swearing during a visit by one of the bishop's officials. By 1555, the church was without a curate.

Curiously, despite this profligacy, Wokingham can lay claim to two bishops over the course of the next century.

Thomas Godwin was born in Wokingham in 1517. Although his family was poor, his natural intelligence seems to have shone through, and Richard Layton, then Archdeacon of Buckingham and subsequently Dean of York,

This painting of All Saints Church by W.A. Delamott dates from around 1830. The coach passenger seems to be looking with some disdain at the 'loafers' by the wall.

effectively adopted him. Godwin left Wokingham for Magdalen College, Oxford. This was a time of religious turmoil and when Queen Mary came to the throne, Godwin's Protestant leanings made it appropriate for him to find a safe haven as a medical student in Oxford. Once Queen Elizabeth had ascended the throne he turned to divinity. His initial appointment was as Dean of Christ Church, Oxford, 1565–67 and then Dean of Canterbury in 1567–84. He was appointed Bishop of Bath and Wells on 10 August 1584 when he was 67 years old. He was already in ill health, suffering from gout, and after a few years returned to Wokingham, where he died on 19 November 1590. He was buried under the chancel of the parish church of All Saints Church.

Archbishop William Laud was born on 7 October 1573; his father, William, was a clothier in Broad Street, Reading who was a native of Wokingham. His mother was Lucia Webb, who lived in Rose Street; she was the sister of Sir William Webb, who was the Lord Mayor of London in 1597. Laud attended

Reading School before heading up to St John's College, Oxford. Laud rose up the ecclesiastical ranks with the support of Charles l and became Bishop of London and then Archbishop of Canterbury in 1633. These were, however, troubled times, and Laud's association with Charles as well as his own focus on a strict interpretation of the church service led to his arrest and imprisonment in the Tower of London in 1640. It proved impossible to prove any precise point of treasonable activity, but that was not enough to save him. Parliament simply passed a bill of attainder under which he was beheaded on 10 January 1645 on Tower Hill. He is buried in Oxford.

Bell ringing at All Saints Church has a fine legacy. Not only was the town itself a producer of bells, but bell ringing reached such popularity in the 1770s that it became a 'spectator sport' with competitions sponsored by the landlords of the Bush and Ship. The church now has a ring of eight bells, including four that date from 1704.

All Saints' tower stands 80ft tall, while St Paul's spire is 90ft taller at 170ft. The church building itself has been subjected to many alterations over the years; the church tower was added in the fifteenth century, the clock was added in 1817 and the west gallery was built in 1830. The church underwent a significant refurbishment in the 1860s, and in 1873 the present Lady Chapel was added. It was around this time that much of the earlier building was lost to Victorian expediency.

The sorry state of All Saints Church, the opening of the railway in 1855 and the overall growth in the town's population all led to the need for a new church to be created in 1863.

John Walter, owner of *The Times* newspaper and Bearwood house, donated land and paid for the building of the new church of St Paul's. The tower houses eight bells, which were recast after a fire in 2005. The church has a Victorian Gothic styling to it, but its real cause for celebration are the various stained-glass windows. The main work shows the Transfiguration of Christ and dates from when the church was built in 1863. Indeed, the stained-glass windows reflect two major influences of the time, namely the Arts and Crafts Movement of William Morris and the Oxford Movement, which wished for less secularisation of the church.

Walter also provided £1,000 for the building of St Paul's School. A few decades after his original generosity, in 1893, Walter paid for the building of the parish room and an additional classroom for infants on land he had bought at the junction of Station Road and Reading Road.

St Paul's Rectory in 1895 showing Revd Joseph Thomas and his extended family.

There have been Baptists in Wokingham since 1762. A Baptist Meeting House was built in Milton Road in 1774 and a separate Wokingham Baptist Church was established. During the course of the first half of the nineteenth century, the church grew and the original house became insufficient, such that a new building was completed in 1861 and forms the current sanctuary and lecture room.

The church members decided that a school was needed so that 'provision should be made for the daily instruction of children of dissenting parents whose poverty prevents them from supplying a means for their education' and consequently the British School was built in Milton Road and opened in 1841.

The Methodist church was established in Wokingham in 1819. The Reverend John Waterhouse rented a house in Rose Street that had been converted from a barn and which would subsequently be the site of the present-day church and community centre. A second church or chapel was set up in Denmark Street. The Heelas family had a significant role in the life of the Wokingham Methodist Church.

The establishment of a Roman Catholic place of worship in Wokingham did not occur until the twentieth century. There had been few Roman Catholics in Reading and the surrounding areas in the early part of the eighteenth century. Friar Baynham would say Mass secretly to Catholics in the area such as the Englefields at Whiteknights or the Perkins at Ufton Court. Francis Longuet, a French priest exiled from France during the French Revolution, arrived in Reading around 1802 and carried out pastoral work until he was brutally robbed and murdered in 1817.

St James Church in Reading was built in 1840, but it would be more than fifty years until Wokingham had its own Catholic church. The Convent of the French Sisters of the Presentation of the Blessed Virgin, otherwise known as the 'Presentation Convent', was invited by a Miss Johnston of Ascot in 1903 to open a house in Wokingham. Their first residence was '*une jolie et grande maison*' at 21 Market Place, the same building occupied at one time by the Wokingham Club, and by the end of January 1904 the Sisters were ensconced and had opened a school. The Sisters moved out and occupied No. 73 Easthampstead Road in 1907. It was here that would be the home of Belgium refuges during the First World War. It was the father of one of these refugees who provided substantial funding for the development of the school. Corpus Christi Church opened at Shute End in 1911 and moved to a new building in Sturges Road in 1967, which was consecrated in 1970.

The Salvation Army arrived in Wokingham in 1880, having been founded in 1865. However, the early years were marred by controversy – according to the *Reading Mercury* on Saturday, 10 March 1883:

Wokingham was in a great state of excitement on Monday evening last, occasioned by the return home from Reading gaol of Jeffries the Captain of the local contingent of the Salvation Army, who as reported in our last issue, was committed on Tuesday last week for seven days hard labour in default of paying a fine and costs for Obstructing Rose Street Wokingham by holding a service therein. Jeffries was 'honoured' with a serenade on Sunday evening last.

Charity

There is a history of charitable endowments within Wokingham over the centuries. Distinct themes run through the charitable actions of the inhabitants of the town, namely education, relief from poverty and the learning of a trade.

The earliest bequest is John Westende, who by a deed poll dated September 1451 made available eight cottages on the corner of Peach Street opposite the Ship pub for poor and needy persons. This endowment was enhanced in March 1516 by Ralph White from the proceeds of the lease of his house.

John Norreys and John Westende provided an endowment at All Saints for the provision of educating boys of the parish. In 1536 Thomas Godwin, the future Archbishop, was a pupil at the school.

John Tickner was a grocer in London and, in his will dated 5 September 1603, he provided for an annuity of 40 shillings to be paid out of the rents and profits of freehold land and tenants 'for the relief of the honest and goodly at the feast of the nativity of John the Baptist'.

John Planner of Wokingham donated rent from his land in Hurst in 1605 to support the placement of one fatherless or poor child born in the town into some honest trade.

John Meriwether of Tiverton near Bath gave £100 for the purchase of land in 1667 and then the rent from it, for the purchase of cold weather garments for the poor; he stipulated that the garments should have his initials 'JM' on them in a red cloth.

In his will, William Laud Archbishop of Canterbury left an endowment for a 'poore maiden' of Wokingham towards her marriage dowry. His bequest also provided funding to support Wokingham boys to obtain suitable apprenticeship.

The list goes on; in 1654, Bartholomew Bromley, a citizen and cook of London, left money for twenty-four loaves of bread worth 2p each at the end of divine service for the poor of the parish. Although there were roads leading into and out of the town, in general, much of the surroundings would have been criss-crossed by paths. These tracks were sufficiently confusing for Richard Palmer in 1664 to pay for a curfew bell to be rung at 8 o'clock in the evening, such that, among other things, 'strangers who should happen to lose their way in winter might be informed of the time of night and receive some guidance'.

And then there is Henry Lucas, MP for Cambridge University, who, in his will dated 11 June 1663, gave around £7,000 for 'the erection and endowment of an almshouse for the relief of old men and for the upkeep of a Master to be their Chaplain'.

Over the years Wokingham has gained much from the generosity of its inhabitants. The town was founded around a chapel of ease, and it seems that faith, hope and charity have been present in the town ever since.

Selected References

Bell J. (2008) *St Paul's Parish Church, Wokingham.*

Bell, J. (2008) *A Stroll Through St Paul's Parish Churchyard Wokingham.*

Bruce, J. (ed.) (1840) Original Letters and other documents relating to the Benefactions of William Laud. *Berkshire Ashmolean Society.*

Heelas, A. T. (1928) *Historical Notes on Wokingham.*

11

IN LIVING MEMORY

It goes without saying that life in Wokingham 1,000 years ago would have been very different from living in or around the town today.

It is possible to paint a picture of Wokingham in 1019; there was a Saxon settlement, a chapel of ease and a few huts scattered around. This is a completely foreign country, an alien place where we would not feel at home. Five hundred years ago, Wokingham was a bustling and maybe smelly medieval town. The layout of the sixteenth-century town remains with us today, as indeed do some of the buildings. Around 1750 the town was recovering from the ravages of the Civil War and was busy brewing beer, tanning hides and knitting silk. In 1919, Wokingham was mourning the passing of the Edwardian age after the carnage of the First World War and the loss of many of its young men.

Historical records reveal the more distant past to us. But what about Wokingham in 1969, fifty years ago at the time of writing? A half century is in living memory; there are many who can recall the events of those times having lived through them. What about in 1979, or 1989? The recent past is not such a radically 'foreign country' where they do things differently. It is only marginally different from today.

This final chapter looks at the Wokingham before the current era, before the digital age and the twenty-first century, through the stories and articles written in the local newspapers over the last fifty years. Wokingham half a century ago may be a 'foreign country' but one that we have perhaps already visited or with a similar culture. Same but different.

50 Years Ago

Depending upon your perspective, or memory, 1969 was the year of the first moon landing, the Woodstock rock festival, Abbey Road or the Cybermen in *Doctor Who*. But in Wokingham the year started with snow covering much of the south-east of England with the country having enjoyed an unforecast white Christmas. Jason White, a 3-year-old from Feltham who had been snatched from his pram, was found safe and sound in Wokingham by a Mrs Edward (mother of Christine Keeler of the Profumo scandal fame). The kidnapper from Nine Mile Ride had feigned pregnancy to keep the love of the man with whom she was living.

The Wokingham Society hosted an exhibition to attract investment in the development of the town, which was struggling against the competition of Bracknell and Reading. They were attracting trade, forcing some local Wokingham businesses such as White's furnishing store in Peach Street to close. A lack of parking and traffic congestion were contributing factors. One of Wokingham's few manufacturers, Metalair Engineering, announced that it was closing down in October.

The 1970s

In 1970 approval was given for development to go ahead in the Woosehill area, as well as seeing the arrival of the first self-service petrol pumps at the Southrold Service Station, in Broad Street. The Matthewsgreen hoard of Roman coins was found in June. Corpus Christi Roman Catholic church was consecrated by the Bishop in November.

In 1971 some of the fabric of the older Wokingham disappeared, partly in an attempt to modernise the town and partly because some had fallen into disrepair or disuse, The Wokingham Club in Denmark Street was demolished, except for the façade that remains today. There was a fire that gutted the Rose Inn, prompting the call for a full-time fire brigade in the town. The Howard Palmer Bowling Green was converted to an open space playing field and the Westende Almshouses on the corner of Peach Street and Cross Street were pulled down.

Wokingham saw work start on a new railway station in 1972, which was only replaced in 2013 with the present facility. There were ongoing

A busy Peach Street in 1949 with a bus coming along the road. Bata shoe shop and Woolworths are on one side and the Redan pub on the other side.

complaints about the 'one big traffic jam' that the one-way traffic system brought with it, according to Anthony Cross, founding Chairman of the Wokingham Society:

> The new one-way system has come into operation and the Society has seen its fears come true – traffic snarl-ups, a race-track in Denmark Street and the great hazards for pedestrians trying to cross the road, particularly in Denmark Street – etc. Things are in fact far worse than expected. To take only a few examples: On Saturday morning there was a build-up of traffic from Station Road right back to the Bull at Barkham; residents in Wellington Road and the roads off it have extreme difficulty in getting their cars in and out; and the mainstream of traffic through the Market Place, Denmark Street and Wellington Road often proceeds so fast that it is well-nigh impossible for traffic from side roads to infiltrate. While the scheme has many disadvantages, there are no obvious advantages. Unless there is a definite improvement, should not the whole scheme be suspended and thoroughly re-examined?

To make matters worse, free parking in the town was abolished and drivers needed to pay for off-road parking. And then in 1973 came the oil crisis and petrol was rationed, with pumps running dry in the town.

The challenges that the town centre faced during this time are not unfamiliar today. Over and above the loss of trade to other nearby towns, Wokingham's town centre needed significant improvement as there were many derelict premises and the local shop owners were concerned that ongoing rent increases would drive them out of business.

Folly Court, which was once a large manor house on the Barkham Road, was demolished in 1975 and made way for a training centre for the Guide Dogs for the Blind Association. Guest of honour at this year's Wokingham Carnival was Lesley Judd of *Blue Peter* fame.

The 1970s saw, in Denmark Street, the final demolition of the drill hall, an arson attack on the old brewery, and the development of what was to become a Tesco supermarket and what is now shops and restaurants. At the same time, in 1979, The Marvelettes appeared at the King of Clubs nightclub on 5 August for one night only.

The 1980s

In 1980, the Ritz cinema was reopened in a short-lived attempt to gain a cinema audience in the town, as the *Wokingham Times* at the time stated:

> The 180-seat studio will be showing newly released big movies – unlike the old sex films which were screened to numerous empty seats before the old Ritz closed ... And as a special treat for young lovers, there will be double seats in the back row. Admission prices at the new Ritz will be £1.80 – five pence cheaper than its Reading rivals. Old age pensioners and children are to be charged half-price at all times with no restrictions!

This year also saw the closure of the St Anne's Nursing Home run by the Bon Secour nuns. St Anne's Manor would become a hotel and conference centre, as would the newly refurbished Cantley House.

The character of the town was now changing quickly and in 1983 the Halifax Building Society opened a branch. In itself that was nothing unusual but it was seen at the time as – and it probably was – the thin end of a wedge

Children in carnival charabancs outside the town hall on 11 September 1929.

that would see banks and estate agents proliferate and push shops and shop-
pers out of Wokingham.

The present-day town carnival can be thought of as having its origin in
the two annual fairs in the thirteenth century. The following newspaper
report from the *Wokingham Times* is just one of a series of articles over recent
years that have covered this annual event:

> The Wokingham Carnival of 1985 took to the town streets and fields at
> the weekend – and, as ever, the main event of the year was an outstand-
> ing success. From early afternoon until well into the evening thousands
> of people took part and watched the festivities helping to raise valuable
> cash for Folly Court, the Guide Dogs for the Blind Training Centre in
> Wokingham.
>
> The fun ranged from cows on the Carnival Field at Cantley House to
> parachutists from R.E.M.E. spectacularly landing on the field in front of
> an enthralled crowd. Activities started soon after mid-day, when more than
> 20 floats gathered along the streets to be judged by Miss Wokingham and
> the Mayor, Cllr. Keith Cattran, before setting off for a grand procession
> through the town centre.

Cllr. Cattran was particularly pleased with the success of the event because it helped to publicise the charity he is working for as Mayor for the next year – a renal machine for the Royal Berks Hospital which will eventually be permanently placed in Wokingham Hospital.

The procession itself was filled with an amazing array of floats, on cars, lorries, and even a double-decker bus which wound its way through the streets led by Carnival Queen Michelle Winkley. The floats were based on the theme 2001 and no effort was spared as the spectacular line-up of colours and ideas marched past the hundreds of cheering and clapping people of the town.

Later the procession arrived at Cantley Field where, after the official opening ceremony, there were shows in the arena by the Thames Valley Dogs Display Team, the parachutists, music from the Reading Scottish Pipe Band and a training demonstration by the Guide Dogs for the Blind Association.

Carnival chairman Mr Lloyd Windust said: 'We expect to make a profit of over £6,000 for the Guide Dogs for the Blind Association.'

The lucky programme prize – a meal for two at St Anne's Manor was not claimed on the day after being drawn out by Miss Wokingham. The number is 0439 and the winner should go along to see the manager at St Anne's to arrange a date for the meal.

The efforts to kick-start the Ritz cinema had not been sufficient and by 1986 it was being converted into a bingo hall, which was opened in February by BBC *EastEnders* characters Dot Cotton and Sergeant Quick, aka actors June Brown and Douglas Fielding. The building would finally close its doors in May 1990.

Princess Diana made her first of subsequently regular visits to the town in 1987 while, in the same year, John Redwood was first elected as MP for the constituency.

The 1980s ended with the much-lamented closure of Martin's Pool. The open-air pool had been a key leisure facility in the town for the previous half century and would be replaced by a new pool, the Carnival Pool, in the early 1990s. But it was not all bad news as Christmas 1989 saw the first of the annual Toy Runs by the leather-clad Christian Motorcyclists Association.

The 1990s

While many remember the Great Storm of 1987, the 1990s blew in with the Burn's Day storm. Winds in Wokingham hit 80mph, trains were stranded at Ascot, and Finchampstead was left in total darkness with no power. The inclement weather would be a key headline twelve months later when the country was hit by the 'Big Freeze', when temperatures reached a low of minus 9 degrees Celcius.

In 1990 there was the much-awaited arrival of Prince William:

Wokingham said, 'Hello William' on Monday (10th September) as the eight-year-old prince arrived in the town for his first day at Ludgrove School. Accompanied by Prince Charles and Princess Diana, William arrived by Bentley to be greeted by school heads Nichol Marston and Gerald Barber. Princess Diana looked tearful as she said goodbye to the young prince.

Harry would join the school two years later and with his brother and mother would regularly stop off at Santram newsagents in Rances Lane to buy sweets. But as Royalty arrived in the town the military started to move out. The last passing out parade took place at Arborfield in 1992 as the training garrison moved to Pirbright.

Along Finchampstead Road, the Pin and Bowl, a pub dating from at least 1720, was demolished to make way for more houses when the football ground was finally closed.

In 1996 there was the 104th and sadly last birthday of Mabel Perkins:

Canada paid tribute to Mabel Perkins, who celebrated her 104th birthday yesterday (23rd May). She was the first lady of Wokingham from 1937 to 1938 when her husband, Frank, was Mayor. She is believed to be the town's oldest inhabitant. She endeared herself to many by opening her home to evacuees and soldiers during the war. At one time she had bunks in her attic for 20 soldiers and was caring for five young girl evacuees from London. She prepared soup for Canadian soldiers stationed thousands of miles from home and provided them with other very welcome home comforts. The Canadian High Commission also expressed their thanks and appreciation for the many services she provided Canadian servicemen during the war and the associa-

This delightful postcard shows Wiltshire Road with All Saints Church in the distance. Wokingham was a quiet county town at the start of the twentieth century when this photo was taken.

tion she has maintained in the years since then. On Mabel's 100th birthday the Canadian Veteran Association UK planted a tree in her honour.

The links to the past were fading quickly as the 1990s saw a new library, the closure of the old police station, a new out-of-town supermarket and the demise of Wokingham Town Football Club.

The New Millennium

This millennium and century have seen a recurrence of many of the themes that have run through the last fifty years: the town centre redevelopment, ongoing problems with traffic, a new railway station and a continual shift towards restaurants, coffee shops and fast-food outlets in the town. But the winter and summer carnivals still take place, there is a farmers' market in Market Place, and there are no high-rise developments or dramatic increases in crime. The people of Wokingham remain, on the whole, neighbourly, sociable and content to rate their town one of the best in the country.

APPENDICES

A SIMPLIFIED TIMELINE OF THE HISTORY OF WOKINGHAM

Date	Local Event	General Historical Event
c.10000 BC	River terrace created forming the platform for the future town	End of last glacial period
2500 BC	Bill Hill and Finchampstead Barrows	Bronze Age
800 BC		Iron Age
500–300 BC	Caesar's Camp, Swinley Forest	
55 BC		Roman invasion
AD 306–337	Roman coins buried and lost at Matthewsgreen	
c.400		Romans depart
c.500	Woccingas establish settlement at Woking – ham	Anglo-Saxons arrive
708	Papal Bull of Pope Constantine mentions monastery in land of Woccingas	
793		Viking invasion starts
871	Battle of Reading	
1066		Norman Invasion
1085		Domesday Survey
1189		Richard the Lionheart crowned King of England

Date	Local Event	General Historical Event
1190	Consecration of All Saints Church	
1217	Radulphus Rufus loses court case for ownership of church glebe lands	
1219	Town charter granted	
1258	Charter granted for two annual fairs	
1289	First mention of Rose Street as le Rothes	
1294	Death of Roger de la Beche	
1348		Black Death (bubonic plague) devastates country
1422	Roger Wolgrave and William Landen establish a foundry	
1451	John Westende endows eight almshouses	
1509		Henry VIII crowned King of England
1558	Elizabeth I visits Gorrick Well	
1588		Spanish Armada
1595	Richard Marlowe operates a tannery on Emm Brook	
1616	Jane Barber employs an apprentice for knitting silk stockings	
1635	Henry Mountague the younger teaching and living in town	
1641		English Civil War commences
1643	Thirty houses burnt down by Royalist troops	
1649		Execution of Charles I
1664	Richard Palmer pays for bells to be rung for benefit of 'strangers who should happen to lose their way'	
1666		Great Fire of London
1667	Henry Lucas's bequest establishes almshouse at Chapel Green	
1670	Claude Duval hanged at Tyburn	
1673	Thomas Martin's endowment for five schoolchildren	
1701	Mrs Sampson is landlady of the Bush Hotel	

Date	Local Event	General Historical Event
1726	The poem 'Molly Mogg' written by Gay, Pope and Swift	
1755		Samuel Johnson writes first English dictionary
1759	Stagecoach service from Wokingham to Reading	
1756	Martha Binfield is landlady of the Roebuck	
1767	Wokingham beat Henley in cricket match	
1776	Old Workhouse is 'home' to twenty-five inmates	American War of Independence starts
1787	Tom Johnson beats Bill Warr in bare-knuckle fight	
1794	Elizabeth North found dead after mayhem of bull-baiting	
1825	Wokingham Cricket Club founded	
1829		'Swing' Riots
1831		Cholera arrives in England
1833	Parliamentary report states that Wokingham 'has no manufacturing'	
1837		Coronation of Queen Victoria
1849	Wokingham railway station opened	
1856	Robert Trickey opens the Wellington Arms pub	
1860	New town hall built Police force established	
1864	St Paul's Church consecrated	
1875	Wokingham Football Club founded	
1890	Miss Laura Baker opens her school	
1910	The Wokingham Club premises donated by Howard Palmer	
1913	The Electric Theatre opened in Broad Street	
1914	Arrival of Belgian refugees	Start of First World War
1915	Private Frederick Fullbrook killed in action	
1934	Martin's Lido opened	

Date	Local Event	General Historical Event
1930	The Holt School opened	
1939	Arrivals of evacuees from London	Start of Second World War
1973		UK joins European Union
1984	Murder of Mark Tildesley	
1987		The Great Storm
1989	Martin's Lido closure	Tim Berners-Lee develops World Wide Web
1990	Prince William attends Ludgrove School	
2013	New Wokingham railway station opened	
2018	Town centre redevelopment starts	

LISTED BUILDINGS AND MONUMENTS

Location	(Grade) Listing	Detail
Barkham Road	(II) Folly Farm	Early seventeenth-century farmhouse
	(II) The Old Cottage	Late sixteenth-century cottage next to Tanhouse Lane
Binfield Road	(II) Barn approximately 20m north-west of Beanoak Farmhouse	Barn early eighteenth century
	(II) Beanoak Farmhouse	Late eighteenth-century farmhouse
	(II) Cottage approximately 4m north of Beanoak Farmhouse	Cottage and small dairy early eighteenth century
Blagrove Lane	(II) Barn approximately 15m south-west of Hutt's Farmhouse	Late sixteenth-century barn
	(II) Barn approximately 22m north-west of Blagrove Farmhouse	Late seventeenth-century barn
	(II) Barn approximately 30m north of Blagrove Farmhouse	Late eighteenth-century barn
	(II) Barn approximately 8m north-east of Blagrove Farmhouse	Threshing barn early seventeenth century
	(II) Blagrove Farmhouse	Early seventeenth-century farmhouse

Location	(Grade) Listing	Detail
	(II) Cattle shelter, approximately 10m east of Hutt's Farmhouse	Late seventeenth–century cattle shelter
	(II) Hutt's Farmhouse	Early sixteenth–century farmhouse
Broad Street	(II) 11 and 13, Broad Street	Late eighteenth century
	(II) 19, Broad Street	Late eighteenth century
	(II) 22, Broad Street	Small town house mid-eighteenth century
	(II) 28, Broad Street	Small town house mid-eighteenth century
	(II) 29, Broad Street	Late sixteenth–century house
	(II) 30–36, Broad Street	Terrace of four cottages late eighteenth century
	(II) 7, Broad Street	Early nineteenth century–town house
	(II) 9, Broad Street	Late eighteenth–century town house
	(II) Colburn House	Town house late eighteenth century
	(II) Markham House and Front Railings	Large house *c*.1840
	(II) Milestone adjoining north-west corner of the Post Office	Late eighteenth century milestone
	(II) No. 24 and front railings	Small mid-seventeenth–century town house
	(II) Nos 35 and 37 and front railings	Two eighteenth–century cottages
	(II) Nos 12A–14	Mid-nineteenth–century houses
	(II) Oxford House (No. 39)	Town house early eighteenth century
	(II) Pair of K6 telephone kiosks outside Nos 13–15 and No. 16 (Head Post Office) Broad Street	Pair of Telephone kiosks. Type K6. Designed 1935 by Sir Giles Gilbert Scott
	(II) The Gatehouse	Eighteenth-century house
	(II★) Montague House and attached garden walls	Large mid-eighteenth–century town house
	(II★) The Elms	Sixteenth-century town house or earlier

Location	(Grade) Listing	Detail
	(II★) Tudor House	Early to late sixteenth–century houses
Chapel Green	(I) Henry Lucas Hospital and attached water pumps	Almshouses and attached water pumps. Founded 1663 by Henry Lucas
	(II) Garden wall at Lucas Hospital	Around seventeenth-century garden wall
	(II) Luckley Oakley School	Country house 1907 by Sir Ernest Newton in a free Elizabethan style
	(II★) Outbuildings at Lucas Hospital	Charity hospital founded 1663
Denmark Street	(II) 10, Denmark Street	Mid sixteenth–century small hall house
	(II) 2, Denmark Street	Early seventeenth century
	(II) 31 and 33, Denmark Street	Early seventeenth-century cottage
	(II) 35, Denmark Street	Hall house late fifteenth century
	(II) 37 and 39, Denmark Street	Two cottages early seventeenth century
	(II) 4 and 6, Denmark Street	Early nineteenth century
	(II) 47 and 49, Denmark Street	Early nineteenth century
	(II) 51 and 53, Denmark Street	House late sixteenth century
	(II) 8 and 8a, Denmark Street	Early seventeenth century house
	(II) The Courtyard (Nos 22–28)	Early sixteenth century
	(II) The Crispin public house	Hall house early sixteenth century
	(II) The Duke's Head public house	eighteenth-century house
	(II) The Lord Raglan public house	Early nineteenth century
Easthampstead Road	(II) Nos 3 and 5 and the southern section of the Victoria Arms public house	Two eighteenth-century cottages
Finchampstead Road	(II) Southbrook (No. 68)	Late eighteenth-century house
Glebelands	(II) Cottage adjoining stables at Glebelands the cottage	Groom's cottage 1897 by Sir Ernest Newton

Location	(Grade) Listing	Detail
	(II) Glebelands	Country house set in parkland 1897 by Sir Ernest Newton in the Tudor style
	(II) Stables, north-west of Glebelands	Stables 1897 by Sir Ernest Newton
	(II) The Lodge at Glebelands and adjoining wall	Lodge *c*.1897 by Sir Ernest Newton
Goodchild Road	(II) The Annexe at Westcott Infant School	School block *c*.1906
	(II) Westcott Infant School	1906 school
Holt Lane	(II) The Holt	Late sixteenth-century house
Keephatch Road	(II) Dowlesgreen Farmhouse	Mid-seventeenth-century farmhouse
	(II) Keeper's Cottage	Mid-sixteenth-century cottage extended in seventeenth century
	(II) Keephatch Farmhouse	Mid-sixteenth-century farmhouse
London Road	(II) St Crispin's School	Secondary school 1951–53
Market Place	(II) 15, Market Place	Early nineteenth century, formerly Wheatsheaf pub
	(II) 17, Market Place	Small house late sixteenth century altered seventeenth century
	(II) 22, Market Place	Hall house early sixteenth century
	(II) 23 and 24, Market Place	House, late eighteenth century
	(II) 3 and 4, Market Place	Town house late eighteenth century
	(II) 5, Market Place	Town house early seventeenth century
	(II) Drinking fountain, approximately 1m from north-east corner of the town hall	1881 drinking fountain
	(II) Fosters	Late eighteenth-century town house
	(II) K6 telephone kiosk next to entrance to town hall	Telephone kiosk, Type K6. Designed 1955 by Sir Giles Gilbert Scott

Location	(Grade) Listing	Detail
	(II) Roebuck public house	Sixteenth-century house
	(II) Bush Walk	Late fifteenth-century former inn
	(II) The Rose Inn	Early fifteenth-century hall house
	(II★) 6, Market Place	Mid-eighteenth-century town house
	(II★) Red Lion public house	Hall house, mid-fifteenth century
	(II★) The town hall	Town hall and police station, later also fire station, *c.*1860
Milton Road	(II) 12, Milton Road	Late eighteenth century
	(II) 2 and 4, Milton Road	Mid-sixteenth century
	(II) 6 and 8, Milton Road	Late seventeenth-century cottages
	(II) The Auction House	Former British School, latterly auction rooms. Built in 1841
	(II) Three wall and gate piers to Wokingham Baptist Church	Wall and gate piers *c.*1860.
	(II) Wokingham Baptist Church	Baptist Church, *c.*1860, by Poulton and Woodman of Reading
Peach Street	(II) 45, Peach Street	Mid-nineteenth-century forge
	(II) 48 and 50, Peach Street	Early sixteenth-century house
	(II) 52, Peach Street	Mid-sixteenth-century house
	(II) The Overhangs	Early sixteenth century
	(II) The Ship Inn	Early eighteenth-century house
Reading Road	(II) Cottage in garden adjoining No. 40 Reading Road on south-west	Late sixteenth-century cottage
	(II) Garden wall to road at No. 40 Reading Road	Late sixteenth-century garden wall
	(II) Lynch gate to the Church of St Paul's	Late nineteenth century by Henry Woodyer
	(II) Ochiltree Cottage	Hall house mid-sixteenth century

Location	(Grade) Listing	Detail
	(II★) Church of St Paul's	Parish church 1862 by Henry Woodyer
Rectory Road	(II) 1 and 3, Rectory Road	Mid-nineteenth century
	(II) Dwarf garden wall and gate piers Nos 2–10 to police station	Early twentieth-century dwarf garden wall
	(II) Police station	Police station 1904 by Joseph Morris
	(II) Wall adjoining Nos 1 and 3 on the north-east	Late eighteenth-century wall
Rose Street	(II) 12 and 14, Rose Street	Early nineteenth century
	(II) 16 and 18, Rose Street	Wealden Hall house early fifteenth century
	(II) 25, Rose Street	Town house mid-eighteenth century
	(II) 27 and 29, Rose Street	Mid to late fifteenth century
	(II) 31 and 31a, Rose Street	Mid seventeenth-century cottage
	(II) 32, Rose Street	Mid-eighteenth-century house
	(II) 34, Rose Street	Small house late sixteenth century
	(II) 36 and 38, Rose Street	Early seventeenth century
	(II) 4, Rose Street	Small house late sixteenth century
	(II) 40, 42, 44 and 44a, Rose Street	Hall house early sixteenth century
	(II) 46, 48 and 50, Rose Street	Hall house with cross wing late fourteenth century
	(II) 6, 8 and 10, Rose Street	Row of early seventeenth-century cottages
	(II) 60, Rose Street	Early seventeenth-century cottage
	(II) 62, Rose Street	Early seventeenth-century cottage
	(II) 63, Rose Street	Late sixteenth-century cottage
	(II) 78, Rose Street	Early eighteenth-century house

Location	(Grade) Listing	Detail
	(II) 82, Rose Street	Mid-sixteenth-century cottage extended in seventeenth century
	(II) 86, Rose Street	Small late eighteenth-century house
	(II) Dolphins the Cottage (No. 94)	Early seventeenth-century cottage
	(II) Endon Cottage Virginia Cottage (No. 63)	Mid-eighteenth-century town house
	(II) Paradise Cottage the Old Bakery (68/70)	Hall house early sixteenth century
	(II) Rose Cottage (No. 65)	Late sixteenth-century cottage
	(II) The Cottage Tudor Corner (No. 6)	Late fourteenth-century house with cross wing
	(II) The Metropolitan public house	Hall house, mid-fifteenth century
	(II) The Small House (Nos 52–54)	Around fifteenth-century hall house
	(II) Wingmore Lodge (No. 2)	Mid-eighteenth-century town house
	(II★) 33, Rose Street	Hall house from late fifteenth century
	(II★) 35 and 35a, Rose Street	Wealden hall house, and byre, mid-fifteenth century
	(II★) 37, Rose Street	Wealden hall house, and byre, mid-fifteenth century
	(II★) 39, Rose Street	Merchants house late fifteenth century
	(II★) 80, Rose Street	Late fifteenth-century cottage
	(II★) WADE Day Centre (No. 20)	Late sixteenth-century house
Shute End	(II) 1, Shute End	Late sixteenth century
	(II) 10a, Shute End	*c.*1830 service wing to Shute End House
	(II) 3, Shute End	Late sixteenth-century cottage
	(II) 4, Shute End	Cottage mid-sixteenth century

Location	(Grade) Listing	Detail
	(II) 5, Shute End	Late sixteenth-century cottage
	(II) 8, Shute End	Small nineteenth-century house
	(II) Admiral House	Early nineteenth-century house formerly Denton Lodge
	(II) Barford House and front railings	House *c.*1850
	(II) No. 12 and front railings	Late nineteenth-century house
	(II) Parish Rooms	Parish Rooms, 1893
	(II) Railings in front of No. 6 Shute End	Eighteenth-century railings
	(II★) 6, Shute End	Sixteenth-century town house
	(II★) Shute End House (No. 10)	Town house probably seventeenth century
South Drive	(II) 7, South Drive	House, *c.*1908–09, designed by the architect Frank Morris
Station Road	(II) Footbridge immediately south of Wokingham station	Late nineteenth-century footbridge
	(II) Hope and Anchor public house	Wealden Hall house, now public house. Mid-fifteenth century
The Terrace	(II) 15, The Terrace	Small house mid-fourteenth century
	(II) 17, 19, 21 and 21a, The Terrace	Timber-framed mid-sixteenth century
	(II) 29 and 31, The Terrace	Late eighteenth century
	(II) 3 and 5, The Terrace	Early nineteenth century
	(II) 35, The Terrace	Small house late sixteenth century
	(II) 37, The Terrace	Small house late sixteenth century
	(II) 39, The Terrace	Mid-nineteenth-century house
	(II) 41, The Terrace	Late sixteenth-century house
	(II) 7 and 9, The Terrace	Pair of small late eighteenth-century houses

Location	(Grade) Listing	Detail
	(II) Astwood House	Early eighteenth-century house
	(II) Burcott House	Mid–nineteenth-century house
	(II) Queen's Head public house	Early fifteenth-century hall house
	(II) St Clements (No. 11)	Sixteenth-century house
	(II) The Old House	Wealden hall house, mid-fifteenth century
	(II) West Lodge	Sixteenth-century house
Warren House Road	(II) Barn at Ashridge Farm, south-east of farmhouse	Threshing barn late sixteenth century
	(II) Cattle shed at Ashridge Farm, north of farmhouse	Mid-seventeenth-century cattle shed
	(II) Milestone in the garden of Ashridge Farmhouse, approximately 3m south of entrance porch	Milestone 1747
	(II★) Ashridge Farmhouse	Farmhouse from late sixteenth century
Wiltshire Road	(II) Ashridge Cottage	Late fifteenth-century hall house
	(II) Beaver Tomb, approximately 11m west of north aisle, Church of All Saints	Beaver Monument, a late eighteenth-century pedestal tomb for a wife and nephew
	(II) Boundary marker at south-west corner of No. 6 Wiltshire Road	Early nineteenth-century boundary marker between Berkshire and Wiltshire
	(II) Mollony tomb, approximately 14m north of tower, Church of All Saints	Chest tomb of Daniel Mollony, died 1839
	(II) Richmond Cottage (No. 8)	Late fifteenth-century hall house
	(II) Wiltshire Farmhouse	Early seventeenth-century farmhouse
	(II★) Church of All Saints	Parish church, late fourteenth-century tower and clerestory added fifteenth century

PUBS AND INNS OF WOKINGHAM

This list builds on the work completed by D. Ayres and J. Hunter.

Pub Sign	Location	Known Dates
The Albion	Barkham Road	Last mentioned 1880
The Alma	Barkham Road	Last mentioned 1850
The Alma Arms	Reading Road	Last mentioned 1857
The Anchor	37 The Terrace	1777–1910
The Bee Hive	Emmbrook	Last mentioned 1900
The Brewery Tap	13 Broad Street	Last mentioned 1901
The Brickfield Tavern	Spring Cottage, Forest Road	Last mentioned 1854
The Bricklayers Arms	Rose Street	Last mentioned 1871
The British Workman	Market Place	Last mentioned 1881
The Bush Hotel	37 Market Place	1701–1986
The Cricketers	29 Rose Street	Existed in 1901
The Crispin	45 Denmark Street	1840 to present
The Crooked Billet	Gardeners Green	1842 to present
The Crown	29 Peach Street	Existed in 1901
The Dog and Duck	Mathewsgreen Road, Emmbrook	1842 to present
The Dog and Partridge	Nine Mile Road	Last mentioned 1871
The Duke's Head	1 Langborough Road	1791 to present
The Eagle	Peach Street	Last mentioned 1854
The Eagle	9 Rose Street	Existed in 1901

Pub Sign	Location	Known Dates
The Emmbrook Inn (previously The Thatched Cottage)	Emmbrook	*c.*1840 to present
The Fox and Hounds	Forest Road	Existed in 1901
The Good Intent	Peach Street	Last mentioned 1854
The Hope and Anchor	Station Road	*c.*1830 to present
The Horse and Groom	Reading Road	Last mentioned 1859
The King's Head	Market Place	Last mentioned 1852
The Lord Raglan	30 Denmark Street	*c.*1830 to present
Bar Fifty Six (previously The Metropolitan)	58 Rose Street	1873 or earlier to present
The New Leathern Bottle	Barkham Road	1870–1910
The Pin & Bowl	Finchampstead Road	*c.*1722–1995
The Plough	London Road	1841 to present
The Poor Man's Friend	Rose Street	Last mentioned 1851
The Queen's Arms	23 Rose Street	Existed in 1901
The Queen's Head	23 The Terrace	1777 to present
The Railway Hotel	Station Road	1849 to present
The Red Cow	Market Place	Closed 1884
The Red Lion	25 Market Place	1782 to present
The Redan	24 Peach Street	*c.*1845 to present
The Rifle Volunteer	141 Reading Road	1859 to present
The Rising Sun	18 Oxford Road	Existed in 1901
The Robin Hood	Down Street	Closed 1854
The Roebuck	8 Market Place	1750 to present
The Rose Hotel	30 Market Place	Existed in 1901
The Royal Exchange	20 Denmark Street	Existed in 1901
The Royal Oak	3 Milton Road	Existed in 1901
The Sedan Chair	Down Street	Last mentioned 1877
The Shades	15 Broad Street	Existed in 1901
The Ship Inn	104 Peach Street	1745 to present
The Spotted Cow	Heathlands Road, Gardeners Green	Last mentioned 1872
The Spotted Cow	Emmbrook	Last mentioned 1885
The Spread Eagle	Denmark Street	Last mentioned 1883
The Star	56 Peach Street	*c.*1880–1909

Pub Sign	Location	Known Dates
The Three Brewers	3 Barkham Road	1859 to 2012
The Three Frogs	222 London Road	1771 to present
The Two Poplars	118 Finchampstead Road	c.1840 to present
The Victoria Arms	1 Easthampstead Road	1847–1907
The Warren House	Forest Road	1777 to present
The Welcome Inn	33 Peach Street	
The Weldale Arms	Peach Street	Last mentioned 1871
The Wellington Arms	23 Denmark Street	1856–1921
The Wheatsheaf	14 & 15 Market Place	1876–1976
The White Hart	Hones Green	Last mentioned 1854
The White Hart	65 Rose Street	
The White Horse	Easthampstead Road	1882 to present
The Who'd a Thought It	Nine Mile Ride	1861–2003
The Wine Vaults	Market Place	c.1785–1970
Ye Olde Leathern Bottel	221 Barkham Road	1737 to present

MINISTERS OF ALL SAINTS CHURCH

When	Name
Pre–1066	Alured
	Robert
1160	Godefridus
1190	Jon
	Stephen
1220	Hamo
	Phillip
1268	Willelmus de Wokingham
	Johannes de Wokkingham
1383	Robert Chewe
1536	Robert Avys
1538	William Robyson
1546–55	Hugo Wyrall
1555	Vacant
1624–29	John Bateman and William Benn
1629–42	John Bateman
1642–47	Vacant
1647–58	Samuel Stancliffe
1660–62	Rowland Stedman
1674–80	Robert Salisbury
1680–1726	Benjamin Moody

When	Name
1726–43	Thomas Neale
1744–81	William Pennington
1781–1818	William Bemner
1819–72	Thomas Morres
1873–1904	Edward Sturges
1904–33	Bertram Long
1933–51	Gordon Kenworthy
1951–69	Frederick Steer
1969–81	Kenneth Martin
1981–96	Brian Bailey
1997 to date	David Hodgson

THE STREETS OF WOKINGHAM

This section is taken directly from *The Wokingham Historian, Vols 1 and 2* in 1993. The original compilation was edited by Roger Hosking.

Aggisters Lane	An aggister was an officer in charge of cattle taken in to graze for payment, but the lane may have been named after a man who had that surname.
Alderman Willey Close	Station Road dentist. Mayor in 1951.
Ashridge	Possibly from the Old English 'Hasherugg', an ash tree ridge. The name was 'Ashrigge' in the fourteenth century.
Ayres Grove	Dennis Ayres (1921–98) was a noted Wokingham historian who wrote many articles about the town and who co-authored *The Inns and Public Houses of Wokingham*.
Barret Crescent	A local builder who was major 1935–36.
Batty's Barn Close	Built on the site of Batty's Barn Farm, presumably owned by a farmer of that name.
Bean Oak Road	On the site of the former farm of that name. English names incorporating 'ean' normally indicate field where beans were grown.
Bell Foundry Lane	There was a foundry in the town in Broad Street in the fifteenth–seventeenth centuries, but not in Bell Foundry Lane. That used to be called Bellfounders Farm Lane because the Landon family, the fifteenth-century bellfounders, had a farm there.

Beaver Place	The Beaver monument stands in the churchyard of All Saints' Parish Church near the west gate. It was erected by Benjamin Beaver between the years 1785 and 1789 as a permanent record of the Beaver family.
Bigshotte Rails	Probably from an Old English personal name 'Bigca' or 'Bigfrith' and 'raille' – a small rectangular earthwork. It was a deer park before 1815.
Biscoe Way	William Earle Biscoe (1813–95), son of Revd Thomas George Tyndale and Mary-Anne Earle, inherited The Elms on Broad Street through his mother. He changed his name from Tyndale to Biscoe on inheriting Holton Park in Oxfordshire through his maternal grandmother Anne Biscoe, wife of Timothy Hare Earle.
Bill Hill	Possibly from Old English 'bullynge; 'above the bank'.
Blagrove Lane	Possibly from Old English 'blacan grafta'; a black pit or ditch. It was Blackgrove Lane in the 1920s but may have been associated with the prominent Reading Blagrove family.
Bowyer Crescent	Pet shop owner, Mayor in 1950 who was presented with Freedom of the Borough in 1973.
Brimblecombe Close	Brimblecombe and his brother ran the local coach company. He was Mayor in 1954.
Broad Street	Was originally High Street but became Broad Street as a better description around 1600. Until the nineteenth century the name also included the south side of Shute End.
Buchanan Drive	From Professor Sir Colin Buchanan, the international expert on traffic management and the Wokingham Society's first president. He described Wokingham as 'a town beset with traffic'.
Buckhurst	In 1187 it was called Beechwood. Buckhurst Manor house was built on an estate that existed as early as the fourteenth century. A later house on the same site was occupied by the draper William Heelas and afterwards by Charles Townsend Murdoch JP. Later it became St Anne's Nursing and Convalescent Home. It is currently a hotel named Hilton St Anne's Manor.

Cammell Close	In 1891 Bernard Edward Cammell and his wife Evelyn were living at Folly Court. He was an artist whose work is held in the National Gallery. Bernard's wife Evelyn Jane Cammell, *née* Wellesley, was the great-granddaughter of Garrett Wellesley, first Earl of Mornington, and the grand-niece of his son Arthur Wellesley, the first Duke of Wellington.
Cheeseman Close	Mayor in 1943.
Clifton Road	Mr Ellison Clifton was clerk to the council for many years.
Cockpit Lane	A path that ran to the site of the cockfighting area, which lay behind the Red Lion in the eighteenth and nineteenth centuries.
Coppid Beech Lane	From 'copped' meaning pollarded, having the top cut to generate rapid new growth out of reach of cattle or deer.
Corfield Green	Named after the Hon. Mrs Corfield OBE, a former lady-in-waiting, who was Mayor in 1947–49.
Crail Street	Ian Crail was Mayor in 1972.
Cross Street	This was called Rosemary Lane or Beechey's Lane at various times in the nineteenth century. It was the Berkshire–Wiltshire until 1845 and part of the town boundary until 1885.
Culver Close	Cecil Culver (1910–2009) served as manager for Reeves Removals and in his spare time he sang in a glee club. Although not a historian, he had an excellent memory and provided valuable information about life in Wokingham during the 1920s and '30s.
Curl Way	Dr Curl, a GP, whose surgery was in the Market Place. He was Mayor in 1934.
Daubeny Close	In 1881 Folly Court was occupied by St John Edward Daubeny, his wife Eliza and their four daughters. Lt Col Daubeny had a distinguished military career, serving in the 109th Regiment from 1864 and the 38th Foot in Bombay. Lt Col Daubeny died on 5 July 1921.
Denmark Street	Originally and logically Down Street, which was originally 'le don' street meaning 'hill street'. It was given its present name in 1863 when Princess Alexandra of Denmark came to England to marry the future King Edward VII.
Denton Road	Named after W. Denton, builder and woodworker, whose works were on the site of the present fire station.
The Devil's Highway	The medieval name for the visible stretches of the Roman road from Staines to Silchester. Traces of the line of the road can be seen near Crowthorne and Finchampstead.

De Vitre Green	After the De Vitre family who lived at Keephatch House.
Earle Crescent	Timothy Hare Earle (1737–1816) bought Swallowfield Park in the late eighteenth century and, on his death in 1816, the estate passed to his son Timothy Hare Altabon Earle (1779–1836). T.H.A. Earle lived at Swallowfield Park until 1820, when the depreciation of his West Indian holdings necessitated its sale. He moved to The Elms in Broad Street and died there, unmarried, in 1836.
Eamer Crescent	This is named after Harry Eamer (1887–1916). He was Private 8532, 'A' Company, 2nd Battalion Royal Berkshire Regiment (Princess Charlotte of Wales Regiment). He was killed in action on 1 July and is commemorated at the Thiepval Memorial.
Easthampstead Road	Variously known during the nineteenth century as Bagshot Lane, Shepherds Lane or Star Lane (and started opposite the Star pub). The Old English meaning is 'homestead by the gates'.
Eastheath Avenue	The area between the Emm and Evendons Lane and from the Guildford railway line to Barkham Road was originally the East Heath, one of the many heathlands to the south of Wokingham. East Heath Farm lay in Molly Millars Lane.
Ellison Way	Was named for the last Miss Ellison who lived in The Elms in Broad Street. She intended that Elms Field should be for the people of Wokingham for their enjoyment and leisure forever.
Elms Road	Named after The Elms building in Broad Street.
Emmbrook Road	Named after the Emm Brook. In the eighteenth century it was referred to as Marlowe's Brook, possible because a Richard Marlowe had a tannery on the Pin and Bowl public house site in the late seventeenth century. The name Emm Brook first appeared in the nineteenth century.
Eustace Crescent	Named after Rear Admiral John Bridges Eustace of Admiral's House Shute End, Mayor in 1923–27. Redeveloped and renamed Phoenix Avenue.
Evendons Lane	The village of Evendon existed in the thirteenth century before the new town of Wokingham was built. From Old English 'Yfenedon'. 'Efen' means flat or level and 'dunn' means hill.

Farbrother	Mr Jessie Farbrother was the creator of a flying machine in 1909 in which he persuaded a number of people of Wokingham to invest considerable sums. The large craft resembled a huge fish and was nicknamed 'The Wokingham Whale'. It never flew. There are two endings to the tale. The first was that the 'Whale' was last seen en route to Windsor to have an engine fitted. The second was that the 'Whale' was destroyed in a fire that also took the life of Mr Farbrother, who was never seen again.
Finchampstead Road	Has been known as Blackwater Road, the Brook (after the Emm), College Road (leading to Wellington College) and at one time Hartford Bridge Road.
Fishponds Road	In the nineteenth century there were three fishponds nearby on East Heath Farm. These were old clay pits.
Folly Avenue	Folly Court House was built in the 1860s on land owned by Edward Lane, a farmer who lived in Folly Farm directly across the Barkham Road. The first occupant was Edward's daughter, Sarah. After more than 100 years of use as a private residence, the original house was demolished in the 1970s when the land and buildings were taken over by the Guide Dogs for the Blind Association.
Forest Road	The road that ran through the forest to Windsor and formed part of the Windsor Turnpike.
Forge Grove	George Forge (1889–1916) had been a prominent member of Emmbrook Cricket Club. During the First World War, as a sergeant, he was killed in action on 18 August 1916 while leading a bombing party up a German trench.
Frogmore Drive	A house called Frog Hall was situated in the eighteenth century about where the Three Frogs is now. Possibly originally named from the Old English 'foro', an island in a marsh, or from a heraldic device associated with Frog Hall.
Fulbrook Close	After Walter C. Fulbrook, Mayor in 1944.
Gipsy Lane	Probably from where the Romanies camped, or possibly from Old English 'gypsey' – an intermittent stream. The lane was noted for its springs and wet areas. It was the boundary road for Langborough, one of the town's medieval common fields. There was a windmill there in the sixteenth century. It was called Langborough Lane in the sixteenth century and the name Gipsy Lane was not used until the mid-eighteenth century.
Glebeland Road	Named after the glebe land of All Saints in which it was built. In medieval and later times the glebe land was farmed by the vicar as part of his living.

Goddard Crescent	Charles Goddard (1861–1946) was a police superintendent. He was awarded the King's Police Medal in 1924, particularly for services during the First World War, in which he set up a force of special constables to act in the event of a hostile aircraft invasion. He was one of the officers who investigated the disappearance of Agatha Christie in 1926. His colleagues were convinced that she was dead but Goddard, being aware of her marital problems, was convinced that she was alive and would return in her own good time, which she did.
Goodchild Road	Named after Willliam Goodchild, Mayor of Wokingham 1888.
Gorrick Square	Probably named for Gorrick Wood, which was planted in the nineteenth century. Possibly derived from Old English 'gor', meaning mud!
Grover Avenue	Alfred Henry Grover lived at Toutley Hall Bungalow. After originally being listed as missing, hopes were dashed as he died on 7 September 1944, aged 21, in the Western Europe Campaign and is buried at Lille Southern Cemetery. He was a driver in the Royal Army Service Corps.
Headington Drive	Commemorates the Headington family who owned the Wellington Brewery until it was taken over in 1920. The brewery stood on the site now taken up by a multi-storey car park.
Heelas Road	A famous name in the town – the family owned an emporium that extended over the north side of Market Place.
Herons Way	Daniel Norton Heron was a wine and spirit merchant in the Market Place, he was mayor in 1908–09.
Highfield Close	Built on the site of High Field House, a descriptive name. Wokingham's sole Neolithic find, a magnificent stone axe, was found here. It now resides in the Reading Museum.
Holt Lane	Named after The Holt, a large house in the lane and now The Holt School. The name, which means a wood, can be traced back to the sixteenth century.
Howard Road	This and the nearby park were named after Howard Palmer, a great benefactor of the town in the early part of the twentieth century. It was earlier known as Langborough Walk.
Howard Park	The site of the former Howard Palmer bowling club.
Hughes Road	Edwin Hughes was a local builder who was Mayor in 1901–02.

Keephatch Road	After Keephatch Farm and later Keephatch House, one-time residence of the De Vitre family.
Langborough Road	Named after the former common field into which it was built. The name may have referred to a long barrow that once existed there, but equally it may have referred to the long hill as it would appear from the south.
Laud Way	Commemorates Archbishop Laud, whose mother lived in Rose Street in the sixteenth century.
Lawrence Close	Norman Lawrence was a councillor for many years and in 1946 he was Wokingham's only Labour Mayor.
Longs Way	Named to commemorate Canon Revd Bertram Long, Rector of All Saints, who wrote the *Records of the Church and the Parish of Wokingham*. He was buried at the rectory, where Suffolk Lodge now stands.
Luckley Path	One of the paths that radiate from the town centre, in this case to the site of Luckley House (named Tangleys in the fifteenth century) that stood on what are now the playing fields of Luckley School. It was known as Ifould's Path in the early twentieth century: Ifould was a shopkeeper in the town.
Marks Road	Charles Marks was surveyor and sanitary engineer to the Corporation.
Martins Drive	Named after the former Mayor and Freeman of the Borough William Martin, who tried to persuade the borough council to build a swimming pool for the town. Having failed, he built a private pool for himself and threw it open to the public. The council later purchased Martin's Pool.
Mill Close	This was built on the grounds of the old paper and corn mills on the Emm Brook. The mills were part of a small industrial estate in the nineteenth century. This may also have been the site of mills as early as the thirteenth century. The diversion of the Emm to form the mill stream may still be seen.
Milton Road	Previously this road was called Nonsuch Lane but was renamed after the poet in the middle of the nineteenth century.
Moles Close	Frank Moles was Mayor of the borough in 1958–59.
Montague House	Named after the Mountague family. Henry Mountague senior and junior lived on the site and had a school in the seventeenth century.

Morres Grove	Commander Elliott Morres, RN (1794–1884) of Matthewsgreen, served in the Royal Navy during the Napoleonic Wars. He took a leading role in the rebuilding of the parish almshouses and in the restoration of All Saints Church. The west window of All Saints' Church was inserted in his memory.
Mylne Square	Alderman Henry Mylne was a JP and lived in Field House, Gipsy Lane. He was the Mayor of the borough in 1914–15.
Molly Millars Lane	Not to be confused with Molly Mogg, Molly Millar was a local character who lived nearby. The name first appeared on the tithe survey of 1842.
Mower Close	After William Mower, Mayor in 1894.
Murdoch Road	Named after Charles Townsend Murdoch, JP, at one time MP for Reading.
Neville Close	Four members of the Neville family served as High Steward of Wokingham.
Nicholson Drive	Edward Nicholson (1825–85) purchased the Matthewsgreen Estate in 1877 on retirement, having made his fortune in linoleum. He and his wife Sophia took up residence at Matthewsgreen House, now known as Cantley House Hotel.
Nine Mile Ride	The longest of the rides built through Windsor Forest by Queen Anne and King George III. It is said that some of the rides were built by Queen Anne so that she could hunt in a coach, and others by George III to give his soldiers something to do after the Battle of Culloden.
Norreys Avenue and Norreys Estate	John Norreys was in 1443 one of the co-founders of the chantry chapel of St Mary (since destroyed) in All Saints Church. Norreys Farm, on the site of which the estate is built, existed from the fifteenth century until after the Second World War.
Oxford Road	Known as Station Lane about 1864, it became Havelock Road about 1877 and Oxford Road by 1899.
Pages Croft	The seventeenth-century name of a small field situated further down Easthampstead Road.
Palmer School Road	The Palmer Schools were charity schools funded from the wills of Charles and Martha Palmer in 1711 and 1713.
Peach Street	Known as le Beche Street in the fourteenth century, possibly after the local Beche family. It became Peak Street in the eighteenth century and Peach Street before 1850.

Penny Row	Revd William Charles Penny (1809–98) of Shute End, was medical officer, bursar and Professor of Chemistry at Wellington College; he was also a naturalist who wrote numerous articles. Revd Penny lived at Shute End House.
Perkins Way	Frank Perkins lived in Colbourne House in Broad Street. He was Mayor in 1937.
Phillips Close	George Thorne Phillips (1860–1923) served as a councillor for the borough of Wokingham for more than twenty years from 1885 and was twice Mayor.
Piggott Court and Piggott Road	Commemorates Dr Phyllis Piggott, who was Mayor in 1962 when Wokingham was visited by Queen Elizabeth II.
Plough Lane	The original Plough, a beer shop, stood on the corner until the 1920s when it became a public house and was moved to its present site.
Potter Drive	Frank Potter from Emmbrook was born in 1899. He joined the Royal Navy and served as boy first class on board HMS *Hampshire*. The ship was carrying Lord Kitchener from Orkney on a diplomatic mission to Russia when it struck a mine laid by German submarine U-75 and rapidly sank, in stormy conditions, within 2 miles of Orkney's north-west shore. Frank was one of the 723 crew members who lost their lives – only twelve survived. Frank was one of the six Potter brothers who served in that war, three were killed: Frank, Thomas and George.
Priest Avenue	Albert Ebenezer Priest of Sturges Road was a long-serving councillor and was Mayor in 1929–32.
Queen's Terrace	A street that has now vanished. It was where there is now a supermarket car park, off Rose Street. Originally named Lewis Alley in 1843 by the builders Stephen and William Lewis, the name was changed to Rose Alley, Chubb's Row and later Queen's Terrace.
Rances Lane	Reputed to have been named after the Rance family, who were licensees of the Plough for more than fifty years from the middle of the nineteenth century onwards.
Readwin Crescent	Thomas Allison Readwin (d.1889) of Rose Street was a school teacher who ran a boarding and day school for young gentlemen. In 1845 he wrote *An Account of the Charities of the Town and Parish of Wokingham*. Every Christmas he paid for dinner for the poor of Wokingham.
Rectory Road	This road laid out in the glebe lands of All Saints in the late nineteenth century and named for the first house built there, the Rectory of All Saints.

Reeves Way	Ernest Reeve, JP, Mayor in 1939–42, Honorary Freeman of the Borough, came of a family that moved from London to run Reeves Removals.
Rose Street	The oldest known street in Wokingham. Originally le Rothes Street (Norman and Anglo-Saxon for 'the street in the clearing', an early example of Franglais). About 1893 it was temporarily named Queen Street in honour of Queen Victoria.
Shefford Crescent	William Shefford was a farmer at the Norreys Barn Farm.
Shute End	From the Anglo-Saxon 'shete' – the land that stands out – a name given to The Terrace side of the road before 1300. About 1600 the name became Shete End and was later applied to both sides of the road. It became Shute End in the eighteenth century.
Simons Lane	The Simon family owned land here in the early eighteenth century.
Skinner Drive	Edmund Becher Skinner lived at Toutley Hall (in what is now Old Forest Road) in the first half of the twentieth century. He was recorded as a lieutenant with the Royal Garrison Artillery 1914–22 and was later general manager or chairman of various rubber companies. It was during his time at Toutley Hall before the Second World War that anybody who had fallen ill in the village of Emmbrook was offered fruit and vegetables from the garden there.
Soldiers Rise	This is said to be in memory of Richard Lockhart, a soldier in the Scots Greys who collapsed and died there while on a training exercise in the middle of the nineteenth century. His tombstone can still be seen in the cemetery of the Baptist Church.
Starmead Drive	Built in the ground of a large late nineteenth-century house of that name.
Station Road	This was given its present name after the railway came to Wokingham in 1849. Earlier it was part of Barkham Road.
Staverton Close	George Staverton was the Wokingham butcher who in the seventeenth century left money in his will to buy a bull for the poor each year. The bull was baited by dogs in the Market Place on St Thomas' Day, 21 December, and the meat subsequently given to the poor.

Sturges Road	Canon Sturges was Rector of All Saints in the later decades of the nineteenth century. He arranged the building of the rectory, since replaced by a nursing home. Several houses in Rectory Road, Sturges, Crescent and Murdoch Roads were only adopted by the council in the early 1970s.
Tangley Drive	In the fifteenth century Thomas Tangley owned Tangley Farm which was sited close to the present Ludgrove School.
Tanhouse Lane	Built on the site of a tannery that was there in the sixteenth century onward. It was the largest of the many Wokingham tanneries and continued working until 1923.
The Terrace	Called 'le shete' in the fourteenth century, later Shete End and then Shute End. It became known as The Terrace in the mid-nineteenth century after the road had been landscaped.
Thorpe Close	James Egerton Thorpe was the Mayor of Wokingham in 1938.
The Throat	A common Berkshire name indicating a road narrowing or bottleneck.
Ticknor Drive	John Ticknor knitted silk stockings in the early seventeenth century. He was a member of a local farming family and, as a prosperous man, he lived in Rose Street.
Villiers Close	By 1920 Lt Col Charles Hyde Villiers and his wife Lady Victoria had moved into Folly Court with their two sons and four daughters. Lt Col Villiers had joined the Royal Horseguards in 1887 and subsequently served for more than ten years in Africa. In 1895 he took part in the ill-fated Jameson Raid in South Africa, for which he was tried but acquitted. He later saw action in the First World War in command of the Mediterranean Expeditionary Force. Lt Col Villiers died on 23 May 1947 and Lady Victoria died on 22 May 1970; both are buried in St Paul's churchyard.
Walter Road	Commemorates John Walter III of *The Times* and builder of the current Bearwood house in the middle of the nineteenth century. He built and paid for St Paul's Church, the former Walter Schools (St Paul's School) and the clock tower at Shute End.
Ward Close	Named after Dr Ernest Ward MBE, a Freeman of the Borough who practiced in his Market Place surgery.

Warren House Road	Originally part of Waltham Road. It appears to have been renamed after Warren House Inn, which in turn took its name from the medieval coney (rabbit) warren belonging to the Bishop of Salisbury.
Wescott Road and School	Named after Thomas Manley Wescott, Mayor of Wokingham in 1885, 1886 and 1899.
Whaley Road	Ernest Seward Whaley was an alderman of Wokingham and Mayor in 1928.
Wheeler Avenue	The Wheeler family were residents of Wokingham for more than 100 years, serving either as surgeons or as solicitors in the town.
Whitlock Avenue	In 1453/54 a John Whitlock of Wokingham married Agnes de la Beche, daughter and heiress of Robert de la Beche.
William Heelas Way	William Heelas (1776–1856) came to Wokingham in the late eighteenth century as a wool trader. In due course he opened William Heelas & Sons, a draper's shop, in the Market Place.
Wiltshire Road	An unnamed lane until about the seventeenth century, when it was sometimes known as Church Lane. Together with Warren House Road, it was called Waltham Road in 1815. Sometime between 1871 and 1899 it was renamed Wiltshire Road, possibly because it led to Wiltshire Farm or it was in the Wiltshire part of Wokingham parish.
Yalden Close	This is named after Leonard John Yalden, MM (1892 to 1916). He was a private in the 2nd Battalion of the South Wales Borderers and formerly in the Royal Army Medical Corps. He was a doctor's messenger and was killed in action on 1 July 1916.

ACKNOWLEDGEMENTS

The author and publisher are grateful to the following for permission to reproduce material and photographs that appear in the text.

The British Library Board (Harley 3749, ff. 4v -4), p 14–15 Jim Bell for providing access to the Goatley Collection pp 29, 31, 33, 56, 61, 62, 68, 71, 75, 76, 83, 97, 112 and front cover, the Francis Frith Collection 26, 66, 118, Vin Miles for providing access to his collection, p 123 Museum of English Rural Life p 82, NetXposure.Net p 24, 50, 72, 84, 88, 95, 104, 120, and back cover the Royal Academy p 38 and 43, the Victorian Picture Library p 22 and finally Wokingham Town Council for providing access and enabling usage of the paintings on pp 48, 77, 110.

While the author and publisher have made every effort to trace the owners of copyright, they are happy to rectify any errors or omissions in further editions.

INDEX